Victorian Miniature Fashions

Colonel and Lady Osbourne.

Victorian
Miniature Fashions

Margaret K. Danson

The Crowood Press

First published in 2002 by
The Crowood Press Ltd
Ramsbury, Marlborough
Wiltshire SN8 2HR

British Library Cataloguing-in-Publication Data
A catalogue record for this book is available from the British Library.

ISBN 1 86126 485 2

Photographs by Deborah Stone Photography.

Line drawings by the author.

Typefaces used: Giovanni (main text and headings); Tiepolo (chapter titles).

Typeset and designed by D & N Publishing, Baydon, Marlborough, Wiltshire.

Printed and bound in Singapore by Craft Print Internatioal Ltd

Contents

1. Introduction   6

2. The Mansion House and the Family   8

3. Creating the Basic Dolls   12

4. The Development of Fashion   16

5. Sketch Pad   20

6. Useful Equipment for Dressmaking in Miniature   29

7. The Patterns and the Clothes   30

8. The Individual Patterns for Each Doll   32

Bibliography   126

Index   127

1 Introduction

Dolls have been a part of my life from as far back as I can remember. The set of dolls illustrated in this book, with instructions and patterns for their creation, were inspired by my decision to authenticate the Georgian dolls' house received by our daughter on her second Christmas. The gift was received with great glee and continued to give many hours of pleasure for years to come. However, I quickly realized that the house was not built to scale and my husband offered to build me my own 'baby house'.

In my early years birthdays and Christmas were the occasions on which to receive dolls as a gift. I recall that Christmas baby dolls usually came dressed in a knitted pram set, consisting of leggings, jacket and a pretty bonnet decorated with satin ribbons. Generally the dolls were wrapped in a cream woollen blanket made from the salvaged parts of domestic blankets worn thin in the middle and given a blanket stitch edge by the use of brightly coloured wool. I would so much like to have had some of these dolls in my collection but they were made from brittle pottery and, when one fell or slipped, the fingers and nose tips often were the victims. I can recall several trips to the 'dolls' hospital' in a nearby town to have whole new limbs or a head replaced, but I am sure these places have for the most part long since gone. The second

threat to the dolls was for them to be passed through the family to other small relations, once it was thought that the owner had outgrown them. One must remember that these were the frugal, post-war years and many items, including toys, were scarce and often expensive in relation to the wages of the time. It may have helped that we had the benefit of a confectionery and toyshop in the family. I recollect one doll approximately 3in (7.5cm) tall and dressed from head to toe in clothes created from white icing sugar. My father, a baker at the time, had made her to decorate a wedding cake but when she was not needed he brought her home and placed her in the centre of the mantelpiece where he knew my elder sister or I would spot and claim her. After a while I took the prize, following some help from my mother – after all, I was the younger by four years.

I made a point of keeping and treasuring a 12in (30cm) plastic baby doll for which I had spent many hours sewing and knitting a very variable wardrobe of clothes. From my primary school years I had been interested in needlework and the creative crafts. The embroidery stitches and smocking taught at that time each proved useful to decorate the yokes and tiny collars of small dresses. You may imagine my distress one evening to find when I returned from school that

Musical entertainment.

The first house.

she too had been given, with all her wardrobe, to a five-year-old daughter of a cousin. I am certain that this one act caused me in later life to become a first-class hoarder. Since I began to create the dolls this has proved to be a most useful trait. I have boxes and cases full of fabric remnants left over from dressmaking and soft furnishings which span a period of almost forty years. Many of these remnants are of natural fibres – silk, cotton, linen and wool – and thus are highly appropriate for the purpose for which they are now used. However, it need not be expensive to make a collection of similar fabrics if one frequents jumble sales and charity shops. Family and friends may also prove to be a generous source of fabric remnants and other items.

It is well worth the effort and time to cut up the fabric pieces, saving the least worn parts and laundering them carefully ready for their use in miniature garments. I have a substantial collection of ribbons, braids, broderie anglaise and laces, much of which I collected during the years I was dressmaking when our daughter was still small. I now supplement this whenever possible at markets, sales and the haberdashery counters in large department stores.

With the birth of our daughter in 1973 I was given the joy of reliving once again my childhood years. As the first female child to be born into the family for over twenty years she quickly accumulated a collection of dolls. They came in various sizes from a few inches in height to the walking/talking beauty made

by Palitoy. I still have these in my possession, some, such as Sindy and her friends, having extensive wardrobes for every occasion. So we have come full circle: my interest began when I created for my own dolls, continued through my teaching career for the benefit of my pupils, later to enhance the imaginative play of our daughter and now, once again, I am creating for my own miniature house. I began by mentioning my original intention to use our daughter's dolls' house and my husband's suggestion that he should build one to scale for me. How could anyone resist such an offer? Out came the drawing paper and pens and I quickly designed a house worthy of the doll family which has taken several years to complete. I decided to set the family in the late Victorian Age, about 1890, when Edwardian style, through the influence of Crown Prince Edward and his wife Princess Alexandra, was beginning to come to the fore. I chose the theme 'The Wedding Day of the Eldest Grand-daughter'.

My research has taken me to several museums, including the Victoria & Albert in London, the Castle Museum and the Military Museum in York, and the Museum of Costume and Textiles in Nottingham. The librarians at my local library in Totley, near Sheffield, were of great assistance in providing reference books and information to further my research. I would like to take this opportunity to thank the staff of each of these institutions for their courteous and generous assistance at all times.

2 The Mansion House and the Family

The decision to build the new house was taken; this would follow the style of the original and be based on the architectural designs of the late Georgian period. Early investigation of the available models revealed that most of them were inadequate in terms of design and the room spaces available and did not fit in with my first thoughts on the room furnishings. From this it soon became apparent that, in maintaining scale and in providing the necessary space, the house was to become a major piece of 'furniture'.

The next two illustrations show the proposed front façade and the planned interior layout of the rooms which were arrived at after much deliberation and redesign. The room size compromised on was finally settled at 16in × 16in (40cm × 40cm), with a height of 10½in (26.5cm) for the major rooms and 9in (22.5cm) for the 'quarters'. These, together with providing a substantial staircase – since these always seem inadequate in the available models – have resulted in the house now measuring

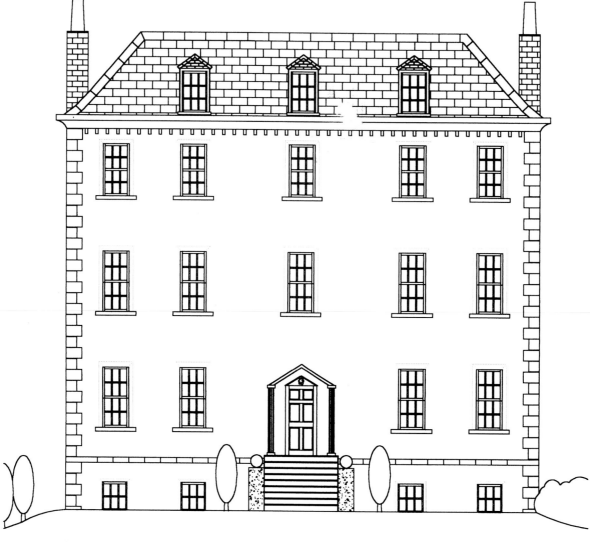

Proposed house façade.

45in long × 18in deep × 52in high (114cm × 45cm × 132cm).

The house has now been under construction for two years. Owing to the fact that my husband is still in full-time employment and his insistence that traditional materials are used, that is, hardwood-faced plywood, no modern MDF, it is not progressing at the rate I could wish for, but, then, I am impatient. It took the winter evenings of the first year to create the numerous windows since the specification was that all should open. I admit that once the main body of the house was constructed I began to suggest improvements. Thankfully, I had insisted upon an impressive central staircase, and therefore to incorporate a further bathroom on the second floor, for the use of the residents on the nursery floor, was not too difficult. However, I then had to devise another route to give the household servants access to their rooms in the attic. I recollected the Victorian terrace house of my maternal grandmother: those were the days of large families and with fourteen children use was made of the attic as a communal bedroom for the youngest siblings. I copied the access that was by a steep, pine staircase that ascended from one of the bedrooms on the second floor. In the illustration you can see this access by the corner door in the bedroom of the governess and the nursery maid.

The bathroom, on the second floor, was inspired by my memory of the one belonging to my paternal grandparents in their Edwardian villa. The only item I have omitted is a heavy black-out blind to the window, and, since my memory came from the late 1940s, I assume that this was an addition from the war years.

House interior design.

Family Tree

Sir William Walter Vergette m. Alice Russell Mortimer
1163 - 1224   cr. 1st Earl following Magna Carta 1215

2nd Earl   Lord Roger Hugo m. Mary Francis de Clare
1190 - 1251

3rd Earl   Thomas Edward m.Lady Anne de Montfort
1219 -1279

5th Earl   Simon Henry m. Isabella Jane Wallace
1224 - 1287

4th Earl   Richard Arthur m. Christina Despenser
1244 - 1284

6th Earl   Lord William Hugo m. Elizabeth Mary Weldrake
1250 - 1320

7th Earl   Arthur Edward m. Margaret Lucy Vernon
1275 - 1351

8th Earl   Cedric Henry m. Catherine Maria Wentworth
1305 - 1375

9th Earl   William Walter
1335 - 1405

10th Earl   Richard Spencer m. Joan Mary Filbert
1345 - 1420

11th Earl   Henry Thomas m. Helen Rose Fairfax
1375 - 1460

12th Earl   Roger James
1403 - 1430

13th Earl   Simon William m. Margaret Lucy Woodville
1410 - 1466

14th Earl   m. Lady Jane Rosamund Herbert
1441 - 1504   cr. Duke following the Battle of Bosworth 1485

2nd Duke   m. Mary Eleanor Talbot
1469 - 1533

3rd Duke   m. Kathleen Lucy Frobisher
1501 - 1551

4th Duke   m. Elizabeth Mary Hargraves
1530 - 1594

5th Duke   m. Anne Christina Fairfax
1562 - 1631

6th Duke   James Henry
1590 - 1621

7th Duke   m. Harriet Grace Burley
1601 - 1682

8th Duke   m. Emma Louise Fraser
1630 - 1715

9th Duke   Charles Edward
1660 - 1722

10th Duke   m. Charlotte Anne Masham
1665 - 1747

11th Duke   m. Elizabeth Mary Cornwallis
1701 - 1770

12th Duke   m. Abigail Jane Churchill
1726 -1784

13th Duke   m. Sarah Constance Paterson
1760 - 1821

14th Duke   m. Caroline Lucy Walpole
1790 - 1863

15th Duke   George Henry m. Christina Lucy Russell
1815 -

16th Duke   William Edward m. Lady Venetia Flora Spencer
1841 -

Alexandra Catherine m. Charles H. Moffatt   Victoria Alice   Nicholas William   Pandora Louise

The bride and family.

Such a grand house deserves an aristocratic family to match it and thus the quantity of dolls grew into the present list of residents and guests who are attending the wedding of the eldest grand-daughter, Lady Alexandra, to the bridegroom, Captain Charles Moffat.

Owing to the fact that I have concentrated upon the making and dressing of the dolls for the past two years none of the other rooms are yet completed. However, I have done some planning and the interior decoration is progressing. This is being done with striped wallpapers and authentic coloured paints but there is still a long way to go. I have constructed some pieces of furniture using the kits from Mini Mundus and The House of Miniature ranges. I am particularly pleased with the result of the dining-room suite in a Chippendale style. I have also completed three needlepoint carpets based upon the designs to be found in *Miniature Needlepoint Carpets*, by Janet Granger.

The Individual Dolls

The Duke	George Henry Vergette
The Duchess	Christina Lucy Vergette
The Marquis	William Edward Vergette
The Marchioness	Venetia Flora Vergette
The bride	Lady Alexandra Catherine Vergette
The maid of honour	Hon. Leonora Kendal-Gaunt
The bridegroom	Captain Charles Moffat
The bride's brother	Lord Nicholas William Vergette
The bride's sister	Lady Victoria Alice Vergette
The bride's small sister	Lady Pandora Louise Vergette
Guest	Lady Harriet Frances Osbourne
Guest	Colonel Edward James Osbourne
The Osbourne twins	Richard William and John Thomas Osbourne
Guests	Commodore and Mrs Andrew Carlisle
Guest	Miss Verity Patience Carlisle
The butler	Mr Borthwick
The housekeeper	Mrs Drury
The governess	Miss Stewart
The cook	Mrs Kitching
The mistress of the linen	Mrs Washington
The nursery maid	Miss Millichip
The parlour maids	Jenny and Kitty
The kitchen 'tweeny'	Daisy
The head gardener	Mr Groucutt
The groomsmen	
Small guests	Camilla Rose Fitzroy
	Digby Spencer
	Venetia Wallis
	Claire Nicholson-Walker

3 Creating the Basic Dolls

It is possible to purchase ready-dressed dolls ranging in price from £10 ($14) to £200 ($280). You can purchase dolls which are 'ready to dress', but, once again, the price range will vary from a few pounds to in excess of £20 ($28). However, the joy of creating, plus the satisfaction of handling a doll that is all your own work, is almost priceless. I recommend that you purchase the porcelain doll parts which are now widely available, and, with a little judicious shopping, for as little as £5 ($7) for a mass-produced item and still under £12 ($17) from individual doll makers.

For my own crowd scene and household staff I had no hesitation in using the less expensive parts, but for some of the main characters I was delighted to discover the dolls of J. Whitehead Miniatures, of Swindon, England, which are beautifully crafted with exquisite facial expression and sold at a reasonable price. I commissioned a set of ten child dolls from Ann Mason, of Dolly Clobber, Southend-on-Sea, England, since I had previously used her dolls for the housekeeper and the butler.

When using doll parts it is customary to construct the basic body with pipe cleaners such that the flexible joints allow for posed attitudes whether the figures are at work or play. This framework is then padded and covered. This, I have found, provides a good foundation for the dressing of the doll. With the careful use of the patterns and instructions given here you can, with time and patience, create superior dressed dolls which will make worthy residents of any dolls' house.

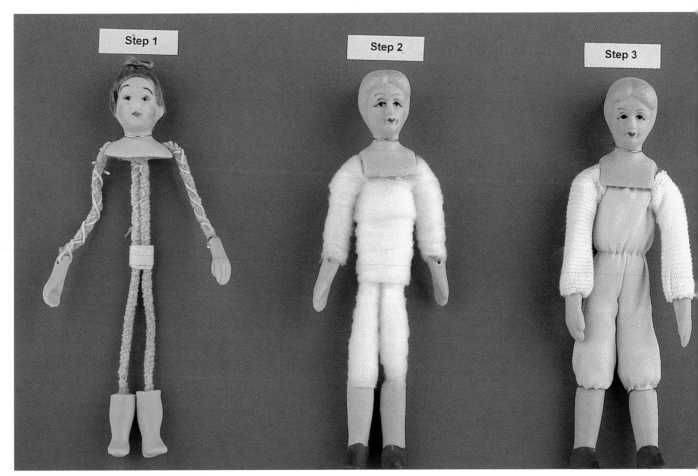

The three steps of basic construction.

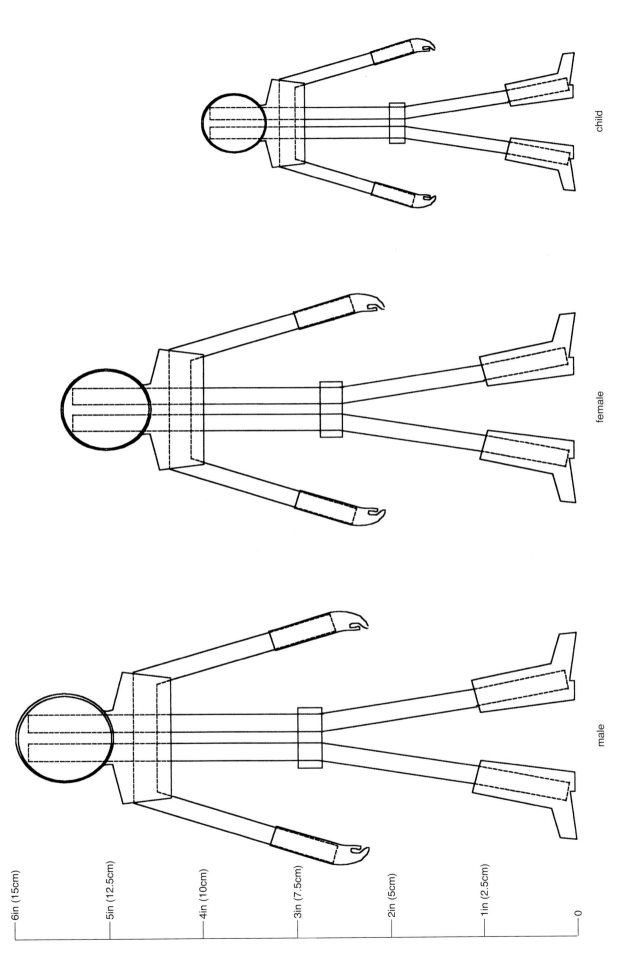

child

female

male

6in (15cm)

5in (12.5cm)

4in (10cm)

3in (7.5cm)

2in (5cm)

1in (2.5cm)

0

The doll height guide.

How to Construct a Doll

To make a doll comparable with the ones illustrated you will require:

- porcelain doll parts (head/shoulders, part legs, part arms)
- pipe cleaners
- lightweight wadding cut into ½in (12mm) strips
- tubular gauze finger bandage
- flesh-coloured silk or similar fabric
- general-purpose glue
- wire cutters or strong scissors

The approximate height of the finished dolls will be as follows:

- adult male: 6in (15cm)
- adult female: 5½in (14cm)
- child: 2–4in (5–10cm)

Just as today people differ in their height, so regard the above measurements as approximations. Senior citizens may be slightly smaller than the measurements given for other adults and variations in the thickness of the wadding will add weight for a fuller figure.

Method

Step 1

1. Glue a pipe cleaner into each leg part and allow the glue to set.
2. If the head and shoulders are complete, thread a pipe cleaner through the two armholes and use the size guide to cut to the correct length (this may vary according to the length of the porcelain arms). Glue the arms into place.
3. Place the head on the top of both leg pipe cleaners and measure the length of the doll. Work out the length to be subtracted such that the doll conforms to the required height and cut the pipe cleaners with the wire cutters.
4. Glue the two pipe cleaners into the head and allow the glue to set.
5. Use the size guide to locate the torso length and glue a length of narrow tape round the two pipe cleaners.

6. Above the tape forms the torso and below it the two legs.

Step 2

1. Cut the wadding into ½in (12mm) strips and begin to pad the figure by wrapping the wadding around the pipe cleaners.
2. Starting from the top of one leg (above the porcelain part), work upward, continuing up the torso to the shoulder plate and then down the torso (providing a second cover) and to complete the second leg.

Step 3

Complete the doll with a fabric body cover since this provides a good foundation for the clothes to slip over.

The pattern is in three sizes:

- the adult male
- the adult female
- children

Use either a soft, flesh-coloured cotton or silk-type fabric.

1. Cut out the pattern on double fabric.
2. Pin and stitch each side and then stitch the inner leg in one continuous operation.
3. Double stitch in the gusset area for strength, clip almost to the stitching line before turning through to the right side and fitting on to the doll.
4. With a bodkin or a cocktail stick, push the lower raw edges into the tops of the porcelain leg parts; secure with a spot of glue.
5. Either sew the top of the body over the shoulder padding or, if there is a shoulder plate, tuck both the front and the back of the body beneath it and secure with glue.
6. Run a gathering stitch at the waistline and gather in to define.
7. Cut two lengths of finger bandage and run a gathering stitch round one end on each length. Slip these ends over each hand, gather tightly into the wrist and secure. Roll the bandages up each arm; this will enclose the raw edges at the wrist. Turn the raw edges at the top of the arms to the inside and secure with glue or stitch on to the wadding.

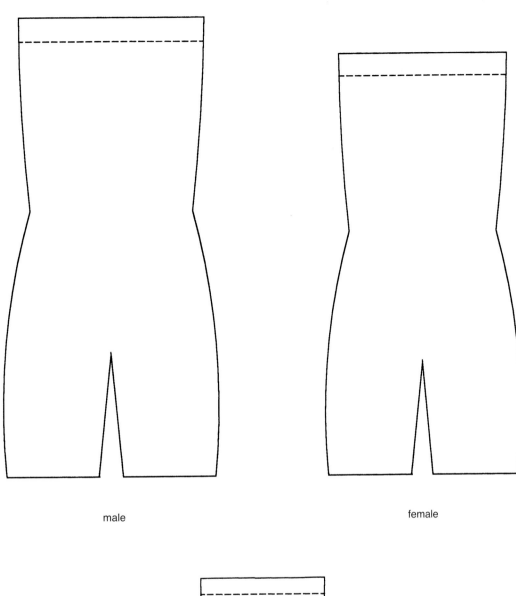

male

female

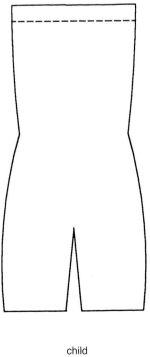

child

Body covers.

4 The Development of Fashion

It is impossible within the space of a few pages to give a detailed profile of fashions throughout the ages. However, I aim to provide a survey of the major garments for both sexes and an explanation for the expansion of fashion, once the privilege of the rich but now within the means of the majority of people. I shall not be looking in close detail at head coverings, footwear or hairstyles.

There is little information and less solid evidence concerning fashion in early Britain, excepting for the occasional leather sandal or metal ornament found on archaeological sites or by accident. The British Isles comprise two main islands situated off the western coast of Europe and we may assume that many fashions were introduced by a succession of invaders who came across the North Sea and English Channel.

The early fashions were influenced by the simple styles introduced first by the Romans and later by the Angles and Saxons who came from northern Europe. The basic garments for males were tunics and loose trousers; the tunics were worn in varying lengths and layered dressing was popular. If trousers were worn they were cross-gartered to the knee with strips of leather or cloth and a belt helped to create a blouse effect with the tunic. The women wore long tunic-dresses with tightly-fitting sleeves over which they wore a knee-length tunic, belted at the waist and often embroidered at the neckline and round the wide, elbow-length cuffs. Semi-circular or rectangular cloaks were popular with both sexes and they also wore similar shoes made of either soft leather or felt fabric.

Following the Norman Conquest the major influence on fashions for several generations came from the French courts. Society could now be divided roughly into two classes: those who ruled and held power and the remainder who were in service to and dependent upon the goodwill of their masters. Fashion was the prerogative only of the wealthy and remained so until the middle of the nineteenth century when industrial development in the western world gave rise to a large middle class, which, for the first time, had disposable income for other than the basic necessities of life. The basic garments – tunics, long gowns, cloaks and sleeveless over-tunics – remained almost unchanged throughout the eleventh, the twelfth and the thirteenth century.

Variations in style were created with differently shaped sleeves in an assortment of lengths. They ranged from the very wide cuff that almost touched the ground to the close-fitting with buttons from the wrist to the elbow; the latter appeared towards the end of the thirteenth century and lasted well into the next. Both sexes appreciated embroidered detail and fur trim on their clothes and also began to wear more jewellery.

The fourteenth and the fifteenth century witnessed the most dramatic changes in fashions for several centuries. Many garments for both sexes became increasingly closely fitted to the bodily form. Male trousers were replaced with woollen or silk hose and fine cotton shirts were worn beneath a short-skirted tunic, tailored into the waist and buttoned down the front. This was called a gipon and it evolved into the doublet of the Tudor era. Over this ensemble was worn a knee- or ankle-length coat, often having a fur collar and slashed sleeves to allow the tunic sleeves to show through. (I think that it worth mentioning here that men wore shoes with pointed toes, often exaggerated to such an extent that they had to be tied round the knees to allow them to walk. I recollect in the 1960s, along with all my friends in college, thinking what a marvellous new fashion this was! How envious we were of the London set, many of whom possessed shoes with 3in-long pointed toes.)

Women continued to wear long, floor-length gowns over which they would wear a variety of hooded cloaks or sleeveless coats so that the dress sleeves were on display. Variations in dress style were created with different necklines that had become quite décolleté by the mid 1400s when heavy gold and jewelled necklaces were worn. The seaming of the gown at hip level was fashionable and leather or jewelled belts were worn to accentuate the style. For a short time the waistline returned to its natural position but then moved to a high-waisted position, a design that remained popular for several decades. From the earliest times women had always worn some kind of simple head covering but these two centuries saw the development of elaborate headdresses. Hats grew in size from the small cap perched on top of a crispinette (an enclosing hairnet) to the wide and tall, heart-shaped hats that were often extravagantly embroidered and covered with fine gauze veils.

The Tudor dynasty beginning in 1485 continued for over a century and provided three kings and two queens for the nation. In contrast to the previous century, the Tudors created a settled and almost war-free era for England, punctuated with the minor clashes that Henry VIII indulged in against France and much later the resounding victory of Elizabeth I against the Spanish Armada. The country flourished, trade expanded vigorously and the increasing population settled to improving their lot. The nobility and successful merchants were granted or purchased country estates and built large houses, requiring them to employ large staffs to manage and farm them during their absences in the cities. An entirely new set of country fashions developed in tandem with those of the nobility.

There are many examples of the Tudor fashions worn by the nobility to be seen in the paintings on display in our galleries and stately homes throughout England. In more recent years the film industry and television historical dramas have enabled us to view many excellent copies. The major influences came from the Spanish and the French court and clothes were made in luxurious fabrics with silk and velvet being the most popular. At the beginning of the period women wore long, full-skirted gowns, either panelled or pleated and these might be opened from the waist to show the beautifully embroidered or quilted underskirts. The cuffs were either narrow or wide, boasting fur trim or embroidered borders, but the low, square neckline was fashionable to frame the heavy gold or jewelled pendants worn at court. The gable hood much favoured by Mary Tudor and Jane Seymour was also popular. By the time Elizabeth I came to the throne skirts were just a few inches off the ground and supported on variously shaped farthingale frames. The sleeves were often padded and quilted but could be close-fitted with a contrasting puff sleeve slashed for decorative effect. Starched, lace-edged ruffs were worn round the neck but these later gave way to beautiful fan-shaped collars which were wired to stand up behind the head – a fashion that continued into the Stuart period, until flat, turn-down collars reappeared in the middle of the seventeenth century.

Male costume was equally flamboyant throughout this period, using the same luxurious fabrics and colours. Common garments included the padded and often highly jewelled doublet, short padded breeches that had extended to knee length towards the end of the period, cloaks and close-fitting hose that contrasted with the padded body. Knitted silk stockings were developed at this time and flat hats with feather trim were popular.

In the reign of Charles I the use of expensive fabrics continued and the cavalier fashions evolved. Long, loosely fitting breeches replaced the padded style, loosely fitting jackets replaced the structured doublet and soft leather boots with deep, turned down cuffs were worn. The tall-crowned, broad-brimmed hat trimmed with ostrich plumes was the recognized cavalier hat. Dresses became softer in shape as farthingales

and padded petticoats were abandoned and the high waistline once again became fashionable. Necklines varied in shape but were definitely décolleté for evenings. Large collars and deep cuffs with lace trim were the fashion for both sexes.

There was a brief intermission to all this luxury and extravagance when Oliver Cromwell was proclaimed Lord Protector in 1649. Sober attire was the order of the day and the Parliamentarians adopted the simpler fashions of the country gentry.

With the return of Charles II in 1660 the lavish fashions of the wealthy reappeared and were strongly influenced by those of the French courts. They brought back the fashion for wearing wigs and there were only minor changes to the embroidered knee-length coat, long waistcoats, breeches and silk hose worn with high-heeled and buckled shoes during the next century. The three-cornered hat replaced the style reminiscent of the cavalier era.

The fashion for women copied that of the French shepherdess with a deep scooped neckline, very full and highly decorated sleeves and an overskirt that was gathered up at the sides to reveal the silk and satin lace-trimmed petticoats. The hair was worn in ringlets with small caps of ribbon and lace perched on top.

The late Georgian and the Regency period witnessed some distinctive changes in both male and female fashions. Men's overcoats dropped to ankle length while the knee-length coat was cut away at the front to reveal brocade and silk waistcoats and giving a full front view of the breeches. By 1830 breeches had been totally replaced by long trousers, but coats of varying length, either single- or double-breasted, formed the essential wardrobe for men. Changes in fashion for women were much more frequent since it was an accepted way in which they could display their wealth to friends and acquaintances. The turn of the century saw a marked turning away from ostentation to the simple Empire-line chemise worn with a short spencer jacket, reminiscent of Jane Austen's heroines. This neo-classical style remained in fashion for three decades before it gave way to the triangular Dutch style, with huge sleeves which lasted for the short duration of William IV's reign.

By the mid-1800s Britain was a prosperous nation as a result of the Industrial Revolution in which a large proportion of the population had moved from the rural areas to live in towns and cities. These people found employment in the mines and factories that were rapidly expanding and developing. It was a time of full employment and, although most of the wealth remained in the hands of a minority, the burgeoning new industries gave rise to the established middle class of today. This new section of society with a substantial income for the first time, required all the accoutrements that went with their new status – housing, entertainment, shops and fashion. In the 1850s Britain was the largest manufacturer of fabrics in the world and this abundance coincided with the increased demand for fashion. It was the norm for the female gown to be made in two parts – the bodice and the skirt. It was quite common for contrasting fabrics and colours to be used in the two garments and there were different levels of demand for flounces and lace and ribbon decoration. The crinoline skirt of the 1850–60s continued to grow in width and it necessitated more and more starched petticoats to be worn in an effort to hold out the skirt's bell-shape. This arrangement must have become very uncomfortable during the summer months and also provided an onerous weight for women to support during their daily activities. The answer to the problem came with the introduction of the whalebone-hooped petticoat – not a new idea if we recollect the farthingale of the sixteenth and the seventeenth centuries.

In the mid-1860s the fullness of the skirt began to be pulled more towards the back of the gown and this eventually evolved into the bustle of the following decade. By 1870 the skirt had become flat in front, but the bustle had increased to such a size, with the addition of folds, frills and pleats, that it became necessary to wear a support. An assortment of bustle-pads and intricate steel frames became available and examples of these may be seen in the Victoria & Albert Museum in London. In the mid-1870s the bustle shrank in size but the gown continued to have a closely fitting bodice which often extended below the waistline and over the hips. In the 1880s the earlier bustle was revived but skirts were shorter such that the feet were visible below them and walking became a more comfortable occupation during the daytime. However, in the evenings trains with elaborate frills and pleats were the fashion, long kid gloves were worn and fans became a favourite fashion accessory.

Once the frock coat was established in 1825 it provided the form that was widely worn by men and, together with a pair of trousers, it created the male suit for many decades, with few changes in design. The coat could be either single- or double-breasted; for daytime wear the skirt was divided into panels but for evening wear the rear panels extended into tails and black was the only acceptable colour.

However, once Britain had become the largest textiles manufacturer men's fashions began to develop rapidly and much greater diversity soon became evident. The frock coat, although remaining popular, became less restrictive at the waistline and shorter in length, with the hemline above the knee. Less formal jackets, much shorter in length, appeared, as did capes, overcoats and even specialist country wear – the knickerbocker suit, a favourite with the Prince of Wales (later Edward VII), a known leader of fashion, together with his wife Princess Alexandra.

Although there were no major changes in fashions for men throughout the Edwardian era, nor indeed up to the 1950s, fashions for women appeared to change on a seasonal or annual basis. Top fashion was still the indulgence of the rich and the couturier houses of Paris, London and New York catered for them. I believe that the Edwardian period was for women one of the most elegant, with slender skirts, beautifully fitted bodices and tailored coats and jackets. The fashion

for large crowned and brimmed hats complemented this lovely silhouette.

Before the First World War there were clear divisions between the social classes in dress but, following the development of the synthetic fabric rayon in 1910, the changes in social structure after the war and the mass production of inexpensive clothing between the two World Wars, it became increasingly difficult to differentiate between middle- and working-class people. The majority could now afford a Sunday-best set of clothing for themselves or at least for the children.

Fashions following the Second World War were much influenced by those shown in American films. Women, tired of dreary colours and of having to 'make do', were ready to embrace a rapidly expanding industry. I recollect 'the girl next door look' much favoured by the film stars June Allyson and Doris Day. My mother wore similar dresses with full, four-panelled skirts, fitted bodice and having detachable white collar and cuffs for ease of laundering. The other option was a smart tailored suit with a jacket fitted to the body and a pencil-slim skirt worn with a crepe or shantung blouse. Small pillbox hats and those styled like a wide hairband with tulle veiling were popular.

The fashions of the 1950s for adults continued to be influenced by the annual collections of the major fashion houses and by the film industry. Clothes and hairstyles were glamorous and Marilyn Monroe was the unrivalled fashion icon until the emergence of Diana, Princess of Wales, in the 1980s. However, a musical phenomenon originating from North America – rock and roll – also exerted a major influence. For the first time the fashion industry emphasized an interest in the younger generation and it has continued to do so to the present day. Circular skirts in a variety of fabrics, cotton for day, velvets, felts and taffetas for evening, were in demand. Several starched white petticoats with broderie anglaise flounces were required to hold out the skirt and I remember that they gave a wonderful swirl as one twirled on the dance floor. Flat, black, ballet pumps with white bobby socks completed the outfit. Young men wearing 'drainpipe' trouser suits were known as Teddy Boys. The jacket reflected the Edwardian era, often with contrasting revers and cuffs and leg-hugging trousers; the outfit was completed by a 'shoestring' tie and thick, crepe-soled shoes. The working garment manufactured from tough denim and called jeans invaded Britain from North America and has never since left. I think it possible that this garment can be found in the wardrobe of the toddler through to that of the senior citizen. It may be argued that this garment was the most successful fashion of the twentieth century but it may soon be rivalled by the trainer shoe, an accessory which has developed from such humble sporting footwear as the plimsoll.

The 1960s were remarkable years for fashion as many young British designers commenced their careers in London. Carnaby Street in Soho became the Mecca for young people from around the globe. The major fashion houses were definitely in decline, once again catering only for the rich, while the popular fashions sold on the high street were inspired by a new generation. Mary Quant, who is generally credited with introducing the miniskirt to the London scene, had a dramatic influence on fashion for several decades. Her mini-dresses in vibrant colours and often having striking geometrical designs were highly regarded and translated into the ready-to-wear market, making them accessible to everyone. The development of nylon and other synthetic polymer fabrics, including the despised crimplene, also reduced the price of mass-produced clothing. Skirts grew ever shorter until they reached just below the panty line, whereupon my grandmother exclaimed, 'You're wearing now't but a pelmet!' Leather was a fashionable material to wear, as was brightly coloured plastic for rainwear. Every self-respecting girl had a pair of knee-high boots with high heels. For the more formal occasion a suit worn with stiletto-heeled shoes, small pillbox hat and matching handbag and gloves was the elegant option. Fashion icons of the time included Jackie Kennedy Onassis, Audrey Hepburn and the top model Twiggy. Many attempts have been made to dislodge the miniskirt from its persistent hold on fashion but it still remains a favourite among the young.

The fashions for young men continued to be influenced by the film and music industries. Two groups who constantly topped the charts, The Beatles, in their collarless jackets, and The Rolling Stones, in more exuberant styles, were a constant source of inspiration for the younger generations to mimic.

The following decade seemed to lose the impetus to produce original ideas, but succeeded in making trousers a unisex item of clothing. Flared trousers with wide bottoms were popular and worn with blouses or tank tops. Culottes (a divided skirt) became a favourite with the older woman. Trouser suits for women became a much-favoured fashion and have retained their importance through to the present. High-street fashion was again directed at the under-thirties and was still influenced by the pop music scene. Abba, the Swedish vocal group, introduced an element of ethnic fashion and peasant costume from central Europe; the beautifully embroidered caftan from the East and diaphanous muslin dresses from India were in demand. Laura Ashley shops revived the 'English Rose' look with tiny sprigged lawn fabrics and broderie anglaise petticoats and blouses. A popular outer garment for the young was either a goatskin jerkin or a coat with an abundance of embroidered decoration on the sleeves and bodice. Jeans and T-shirts retained their popularity and other casual styles were derived from sportswear, such as shell suits and jogging suits with sweater tops and rugby shirts. Platform shoes reminiscent of the 1940s reappeared for formal wear, trainer shoes were further developed as day shoes but 'Doc Martin' shoes and boots with thick crepe soles were the top accessory.

Fashion in the 1980s continued to develop along more casual lines and a trend was forming that allowed individuals to dress to suit themselves rather than to adhere to any fashion edicts. However, there were two influences on female fashion which I think deserve mention: Princess Diana and the television soap *Dynasty*. Diana, who developed her own classic style, became a figure instantly recognized throughout the world. She must have appeared on the cover of every fashion magazine and was rarely off the front pages of newspapers. Within hours of her marriage, copies of the wedding dress were on sale in department stores and women followed her style for a decade, including her blonde hairstyle. *Dynasty*, which starred Joan Collins and Linda Evans, inspired glamorous fashions, which included classic suits with nipped-in waistlines and padded, wide shoulders, elegant dresses with equally wide shoulders and beautiful evening gowns. Both influences had a great effect upon the millinery industry – hats became a necessary accessory and, although fine straw was favourite, they also came in a wide variety of shapes, fabrics and colours.

Everyday dress continued to become increasingly casual and the trainer shoe had developed into a high-tech shoe and firmly established itself as the regular footwear for the younger generation. It would have to be an isolated teenager who did not recognize the names Nike, Adidas and Reebok. Except for formal occasions, trousers, jeans and leggings appeared to be the universally-worn garments with a variety of tops.

The final decade of the twentieth century saw a continuance of casual and informal fashions as the accepted mode of dress. This practice even extended into workplaces where previously there had been a strictly observed dress code. The high-profile sports manufacturers now added casual clothing and further accessories to their products and these were much in demand by the younger generations, regardless of their cost. Wearing the designer label on prominent display was regarded as the zenith of fashion.

It would appear that there are no new ideas as the seasonal fashions come into the high-street shops. Whatever fashion editors may claim, a 'new idea' usually contains an element from an earlier date, proving that fashions come and go in cycles. Fashions have become an entertainment rather than an essential part of everyday life. Today people are more concerned with comfort and practicality and save the glamour and glitz for special celebrations. It is an interesting observation that children, through their own demands, have reverted to dressing as miniature adults during their social activities. It was the custom from the earliest times for children to be dressed as replicas of adults and only when it was recognized how restrictive this was to the natural development of the child was the practice abandoned. Fashion no longer dictates but rather is used by individuals to create a style to suit themselves. There is now such an abundance of different styles from which to choose that freedom of choice is the accepted fashion for the twenty-first century.

5 Sketch Pad

Sketch Pad

Owing to the size of the Mansion House it was evident that 30–40 dolls would be needed to create the illusion of the wedding day celebrations. An early survey of the miniature-doll market quickly revealed the prohibitive costs of purchasing good quality dolls in any quantity.

Once I had taken the decision to make and dress my dolls it was necessary to begin research into the fashions of my chosen period, mid- to late-Victorian. The first step is to obtain as many books as possible on the subject from your local and city libraries. In these you will find all the necessary illustrations for your chosen period. As you decide upon the costume for each doll it is helpful to make an annotated sketch, as in the following pages, to assist in pulling together the ideas and details that you may consider. The sketches will also assist when the time comes to collect together the materials and items required for each costume. They may also remind you to ask your family and friends whether they can supply any of the requirements. You will be amazed how pleased people are to help and to know that a use has been found for the many bits and pieces that they could not bring themselves to throw away.

One example is of how the bride's gown developed from an illustration to be found in Jack Cassin-Scott's *The Illustrated Encyclopaedia of Costume and Fashion*. I liked the swathed apron front of the dress and the lace ruffles extending from the elbow-length sleeves. It was easy to sketch (or it may be possible to trace) the outline of the dress and then I added a deep, square neckline and a lace collar to frame the pearl necklace borrowed from the bride's mother. I exaggerated the flounce of the dress skirt to provide a longer train and added further opulence with a luxurious lace fishtail. When completed with tiny satin bows and more lace edgings, a simple day dress was transformed into a beautiful bridal gown. The circlet of roses and a fine tulle veil added the finishing touches. I committed all these ideas on to an initial sketch which I then had for future reference. The crinoline gown of the maid of honour was similarly inspired from another illustration in the same publication, but again I altered the neckline to be more appropriate for the occasion.

Once my interest in costume was aroused I quickly sought out other sources of information. I knew that paintings of the correct period would furnish me

with extra material, but both book illustrations and paintings are two-dimensional and a more interesting source of information may be found in museums that have costume exhibits. Once your research base has widened it is essential to have at all times a small sketch pad and pencil in your handbag. Few, if any, galleries or museums will allow photographs of their exhibits to be taken. Some, such as the Victoria & Albert can provide illustrated postcards that may be of use. I was delighted during one visit to find one picturing an evening dress by Worth (Paris, about 1881) that mirrored some of the details I had incorporated into the bridal gown. All museums and galleries will allow members of the public to sketch, so do not be shy and make your drawing; it may resemble a Lowry rather than a Reynolds, but the purpose of it is to hold information that you can use at a later date. Embellish your sketches with as many careful and detailed notes as possible while you observe the garment which is of interest to you. Believe me, by the time that you have left, some of the information will have escaped your memory. I can tell you from experience that it is the small details such as how many buttons were down the front of the jacket? Was it single- or double-breasted? Which shoulder did the strap cross? that can cause the most annoyance when you come to study your notes.

Another source of design information is the Internet. There are now many individual web pages which cover all periods of history relating to clothes and fashions as well as sites for national and international museums. These sites contain many useful illustrations which you can easily print out and retain for reference.

The wedding gown – ivory satin.

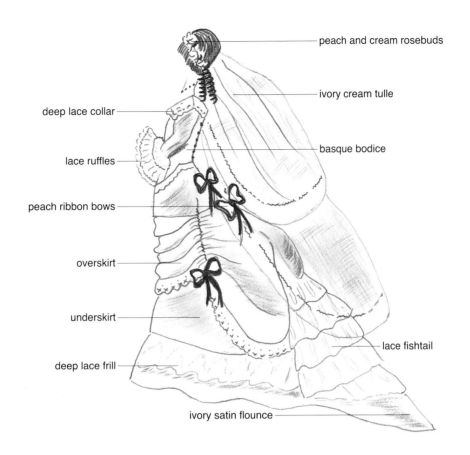

peach and cream rosebuds

ivory cream tulle

deep lace collar

basque bodice

lace ruffles

peach ribbon bows

overskirt

underskirt

lace fishtail

deep lace frill

ivory satin flounce

headdress of tiny rosebuds

shawl-styled lace collar

basque bodice

narrow ribbon (matching or in contrast to dress colour)

three deep flounces with lace inserts

A crinoline gown with tiered skirt,
made of silk/taffeta in a pastel shade.

A crinoline gown of rich tan silk/taffeta.

lace decoration on the bodice

leg-of-mutton sleeves

long tight cuff buttoned from elbow to wrist

narrow brown velvet ribbon

deep flounce with lace trim

A crinoline gown of grey, brown or olive silk/taffeta.

shawl collar in white silk with lace edge

lace ruffles

pin tuck detail on skirt

ivory lace collar

basque bodice

turquoise satin bows

ivory lace ruffles

apron front to the overskirt

lace edging

underskirt with lace-edged flounce

A bustle gown with apron front. Made of deep crimson fabric with turquoise trim.

A bustle gown with divided overskirt. Made of emerald green fabric with gold trim.

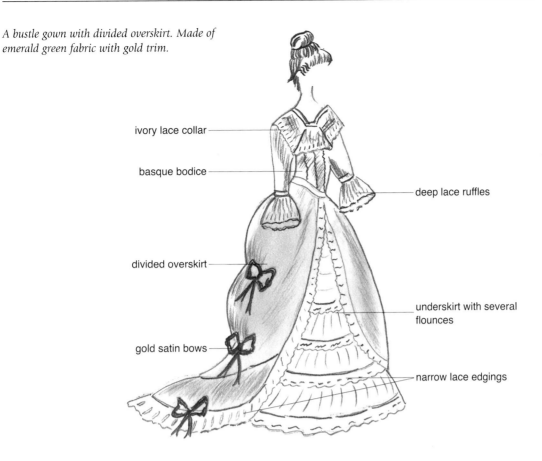

ivory lace collar

basque bodice

deep lace ruffles

divided overskirt

underskirt with several flounces

gold satin bows

narrow lace edgings

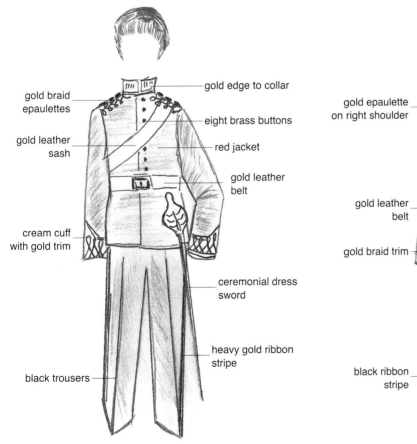

gold braid epaulettes

gold edge to collar

eight brass buttons

gold leather sash

red jacket

gold leather belt

cream cuff with gold trim

ceremonial dress sword

heavy gold ribbon stripe

black trousers

Military uniform. This is a basic uniform. Change the colour of the sash, belt and trim for variation.

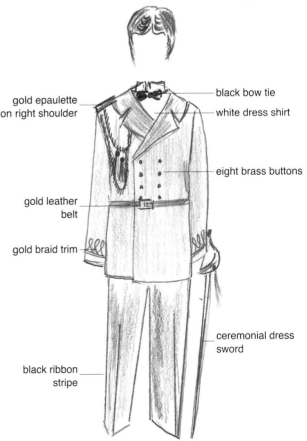

gold epaulette on right shoulder

black bow tie

white dress shirt

eight brass buttons

gold leather belt

gold braid trim

ceremonial dress sword

black ribbon stripe

Naval uniform. Suit made of navy cotton or fine worsted.

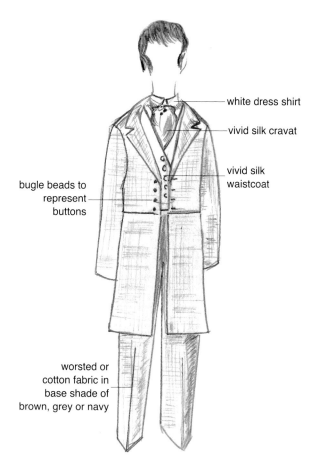

white dress shirt

vivid silk cravat

vivid silk waistcoat

bugle beads to represent buttons

worsted or cotton fabric in base shade of brown, grey or navy

Frock coat and trousers.

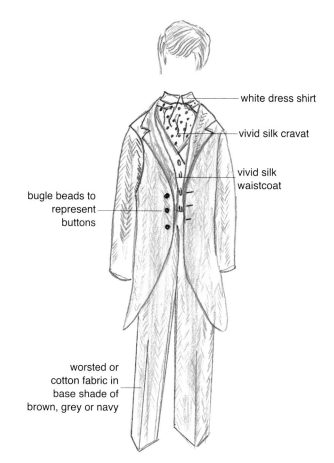

white dress shirt

vivid silk cravat

vivid silk waistcoat

bugle beads to represent buttons

worsted or cotton fabric in base shade of brown, grey or navy

Morning coat and trousers.

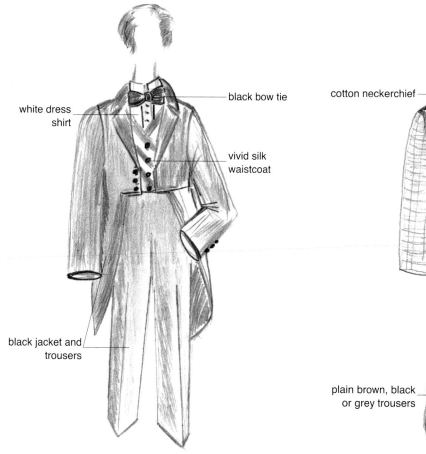

black bow tie

white dress shirt

vivid silk waistcoat

black jacket and trousers

Butler's uniform.

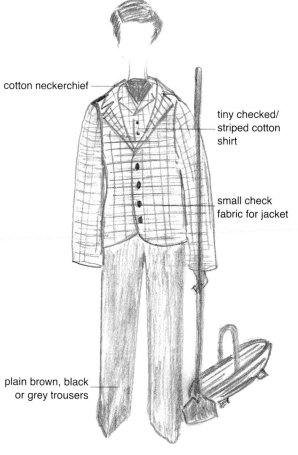

cotton neckerchief

tiny checked/ striped cotton shirt

small check fabric for jacket

plain brown, black or grey trousers

Gardener.

Ceremonial costume.

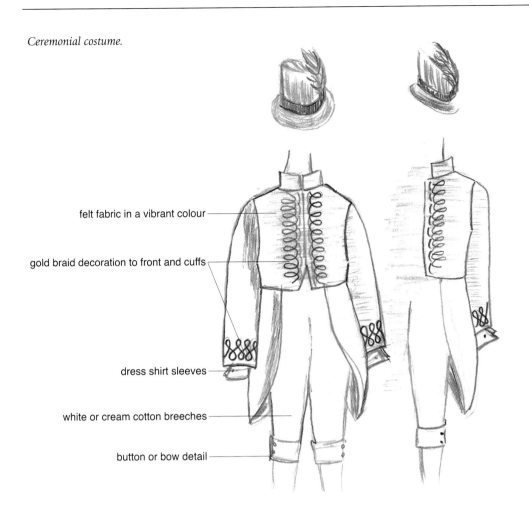

felt fabric in a vibrant colour

gold braid decoration to front and cuffs

dress shirt sleeves

white or cream cotton breeches

button or bow detail

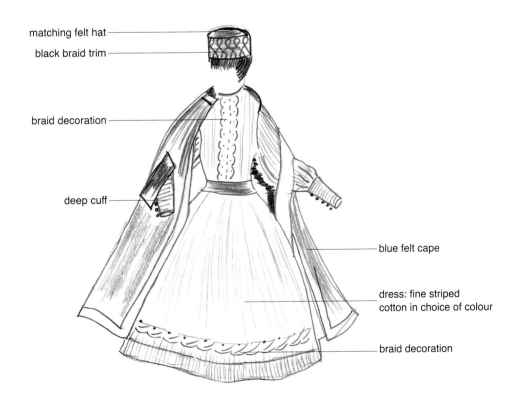

matching felt hat

black braid trim

braid decoration

deep cuff

blue felt cape

dress: fine striped cotton in choice of colour

braid decoration

Governess.

white cotton cap

plain green/grey or blue cotton fabric

decorative stitching

white cotton dust cuffs

white cotton apron

Cook.

white cap with lace trim

grey striped cotton dress

gathered cuff

white apron with pin tuck detail

Nursery maid.

white satin ribbon

tiny floral or checked fabric

white satin ribbon

lace ruffles

white broderie anglaise

Dress with decorative pinafore.

shoulder strap to complete the armhole

puff sleeve/long sleeve (choice will depend on the length of the porcelain arm)

contrasting sash of satin ribbon

ivory taffeta decorated with pin tucks/ivory lace and decorative ribbon

Victorian party dress.

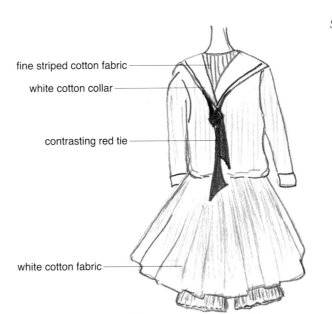

Sailor dress.

fine striped cotton fabric

white cotton collar

contrasting red tie

white cotton fabric

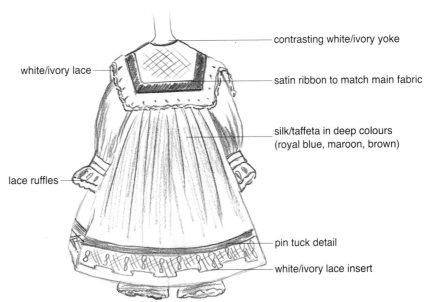

contrasting white/ivory yoke

white/ivory lace

satin ribbon to match main fabric

silk/taffeta in deep colours
(royal blue, maroon, brown)

lace ruffles

pin tuck detail

white/ivory lace insert

Girl's yoked dress.

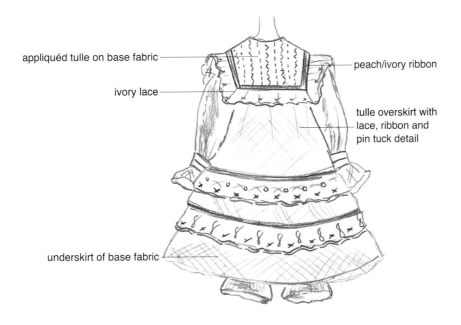

appliquéd tulle on base fabric

peach/ivory ribbon

ivory lace

tulle overskirt with
lace, ribbon and
pin tuck detail

underskirt of base fabric

Girl's yoked dress.

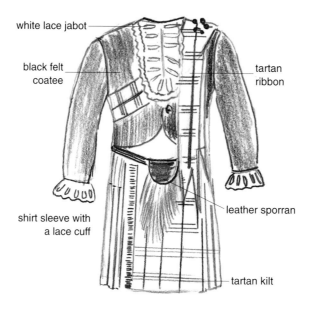

white lace jabot

black felt
coatee

tartan
ribbon

shirt sleeve with
a lace cuff

leather sporran

tartan kilt

Highland dress.

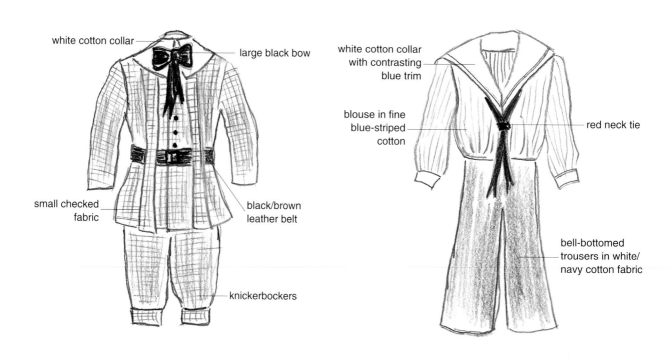

white cotton collar

large black bow

small checked
fabric

black/brown
leather belt

knickerbockers

Norfolk suit.

white cotton collar
with contrasting
blue trim

blouse in fine
blue-striped
cotton

red neck tie

bell-bottomed
trousers in white/
navy cotton fabric

Sailor suit.

6 Useful Equipment for Dressmaking in Miniature

In the early nineteenth century the invention of the sewing machine was the most innovative development to affect the manufacture of garments in that thriving industrial period. The first man to use the invention commercially was Barthelemy Thimmonier, but the man who made an international success of the idea was the American Isaac Merrit Singer.

I purchased my first machine in the 1960s and it was a Singer sewing machine. Although only capable of straight and zigzag stitches, I loved it and found it an enormous aid for creating fashions and household soft furnishings. In the 1970s I purchased what I regard as the Rolls-Royce of sewing machines, a Bernina Record 830. It is still as good as new although it has been in constant use. When creating the miniature garments in this book I used my sewing machine with its attachments and range of decorative stitches whenever possible. Therefore you will find a seam allowance of ³⁄₁₆in (5mm) on the majority of pattern pieces, which relates to the width of the overlock stitch. The overlock seam is used for sewing together and neatening in one operation. It is excellent for attaching narrow lace to raw edges and it also strengthens the seams on small garments. You may only have available a zigzag stitch and I would recommend the use of this with the straight stitch as a compromise solution.

Most bodices are worked in double fabric and it is necessary to eliminate bulk from the seams, therefore the bodice patterns have a seam allowance of ⅛in (3mm). This relates to the distance between the needle (centre position) and the edge of the sewing foot. Adjust the width of the overlock stitch to no.3 on the gauge. However, where it is specified that a seam is to be pressed open then obviously the straight stitch is the one to use.

Other Helpful Equipment

- dressmaking scissors
- small, sharp embroidery scissors
- dressmaking pins
- pair of tweezers
- fabric glue
- Jonco Fray Stop (available at good craft outlets)
- lightweight, iron-on Vilene
- sewing threads to match a variety of fabrics
- doll stands
- a sharp pencil
- tracing paper or household greaseproof paper
- stitch unpick
- tape-measure (preferably metal since a fabric one will stretch with constant use)

7 The Patterns and the Clothes

In the Introduction I outlined my inspiration for creating these particular dolls. However, an additional factor has been the observation that many of the finished dolls available on the market, and, indeed, the few clothes on sale are of a poor quality both in appearance and finish. There are some good quality items but these carry a heavy price premium and are inevitably made to order. Consequently, one of the main reasons in deciding to create my own dolls was to produce high-quality garments which would stand the closest scrutiny, while working within the confines of the $\frac{1}{12}$ scale. The patterns are my own creations, developed over several years. I used techniques based upon traditional dressmaking methods and these in themselves assist in producing finished garments of a higher quality.

My patterns apply to male and female fashions, adult and child, for an approximate period of forty years, 1850–90. At any moment in time the separate generations hold to the fashion in which they feel the most comfortable. Therefore the more mature ladies attend the wedding in their preferred crinolines, while those of the middle and younger generations favour the bustle of one shape or another. In 1850, when Britain had become the largest manufacturer of fabrics in the world, men's fashions began to develop rapidly and much greater diversity soon became evident in the male wardrobe.

In Chapter 8 each doll has its own section with the necessary garments to complete its costume, a photograph, full-size patterns and instructions for making them. For simplicity I have made several of the undergarments common to several dolls and thus the relevant text refers to a basic pattern. Where this is not the case, because of size differences, in order to add character the relevant pattern pieces are included within that figure's pattern details.

It is helpful to read the construction guides several times in order to gain some understanding of how the garments fit together before you begin. It will also enable you to pick up any cross-reference to another part of the book. For ease of construction you will note that all sleeves are attached to the bodice/coat or jacket while the garment can be laid open and flat on your working surface. The sleeve and side seams are then stitched in one operation. Similarly, some of the construction techniques for both the female and the male garments will be similar and again I have referred back to the first complete set of instructions, as they occur within the whole series. Particular examples of these include the pantaloons and bodice for the female characters and shirts and trousers for the male dolls. Tracing the patterns is the obvious way forward and this needs to be done with care to ensure the correct fit and outline shape of the finished garment. The individual sections on each of the garments also detail the method for each of the stages of construction which I have found to be the easiest, although your own experiences will determine your method of working.

The production of a quality garment relies to some extent on the decorative detailing that is incorporated within the construction and also that added at a final stage. Where these are necessary to produce the true 'in period' garment then details are also included within the text in each section. I am sure that, for variation, you may wish to add some of your own, but bear in mind that the dolls illustrated have been created in period.

One of the elements in providing an authentic garment is the use of the correct fabrics, but, unfortunately, these may not be readily available; however, there are many lookalike substitutes. It is worth remembering, as I mentioned earlier, that there are several inexpensive sources from which you might make a collection of fabrics consisting of natural fibres.

As indicated in Chapter 6, all the patterns include a seam allowance of $\frac{3}{16}$in (5mm) maximum, unless otherwise stated, together with the universally recognized markings where these are important for the construction and finish of the garment. Once the pattern pieces are cut out it is important that *all* markings are transferred on to the fabric. This is generally done with tailor tacking and I would recommend that this method should be used if the garment will take several sessions to make up. However, for speed I use the sharp point of a pencil to mark the spots, with a dot to ensure that it is on the reverse side of the fabric and will be on the inside of the finished garment. When a pattern piece is cut out on double fabric the reverse side will always be facing outwards, but on single fabric it is necessary to push a dressmaker's pin through to the reverse side before marking the spot.

I recommend that the simple cotton bodices are worked in double fabric to ensure that the neck edge and back opening have a professional finish, as follows:

1. Cut out the bodice pattern pieces in double fabric – two front bodices and four back bodices.
2. Create two separate bodices by pinning two back bodices to each front bodice at the shoulders and stitch. Press.
3. With the *right sides together* match at the shoulder seams and tack round the neckline and down the centre back seams and stitch. Before turning the bodice through to the right side carefully snip round the neckline almost to the stitching line. Turn the bodice and press flat.
4. To hold the bodice in shape either tack or use a large machine stitch, close to the raw edges on either side of the bodice.
5. The bodice is now ready for the sleeves to be attached in the normal method.

When using finer fabrics, that fray quickly, that is, silks or taffetas for evening gowns, another approach was necessary. I discovered that by fusing lightweight iron-on Vilene to the wrong side of the fabric, before cutting out the pattern pieces, the edges were sufficiently stabilized to enable me to work the garment freely. Normally I will create a basque bodice in one

session so that I am not constantly returning to handle the same small pieces.

It is my practice with the intricate evening gowns to create a full toile garment in a soft, fine cotton (I use old curtain linings which, after much laundering, are ideal) before beginning work with the finer fabrics. With this practice run I can generally work at greater speed on the original creation.

For those of you without much previous dressmaking experience, I would advise that you start with the simplest form of female garment and then progress through finally to the men's since, notoriously, the construction and fit of these items is of tremendous importance to the completed appearance overall.

Daisy, the kitchen maid, would be an excellent doll on which to start since her wardrobe consists entirely of basic designs and, with a little care and by giving yourself time, you will be able to do it. You will be amazed how quickly you grow in confidence once you are holding a completed doll and it is all your own work. There will be some mistakes along the way, but a 'failed' garment need not necessarily go to waste. It is almost always possible to complete with decorative detail and, when placed on a hanger, may be used for display in a wardrobe. Alternatively it may be used to represent laundry in a wicker basket 'below stairs'.

Girls' clothes (see page 100 for further information).

8 The Individual Patterns for Each Doll

The Wedding

Something old, something new.
Something borrowed and something blue.

Although adhered to almost universally throughout the Western world, did you ever wonder where this popular verse originated? I did, and it led to an interesting piece of research with enquiries at both my local and the city library and a search through *Webster's, World Encyclopaedia 1999* – Dr R. Brasch's *Library of Origins*. It was subsequently traced at the Sheffield Reference Library to a weekly journal from the 1860s and attributed to C. Bede. A further line was also revealed but I do not know it to be in general use: *And a silver sixpence in her shoe*.

Marriage has always been of major importance in all societies, the contract often holding more

benefit for that society than for the couple at the centre of the occasion. The celebration of marriage is often on a grand style and the good wishes of all those present are concentrated upon the couple. It marks an important change of lifestyle for the bride and the groom, the end of one phase and the beginning of a new. The preparation can be stressful and obviously apprehension and uncertainties accumulate as the day approaches – we are all familiar with the expressions 'wedding nerves' and 'getting cold feet'.

We associate a special symbolism to each of the four objects, which, according to Brasch, have their foundation in the fears and superstitions imbued in the rites of paganism. 'Something old' represents the values and certainties of the past and it is meant to allay the anxieties and fears felt by the bride, enabling her to go forward with confidence towards an unknown future. 'Something new', usually the

The bride and her parents.

The Individual Patterns

Lady Alexandra C. Vergette	bridal gown	The Groomsmen	ceremonial costume
Hon. Leonora Kendal-Gaunt	crinoline gown with a tiered skirt	Mrs Drury	typical day dress
		Miss Stewart	typical day dress
Venetia Flora Vergette	crinoline gown with a flounced hemline	Mrs Kitching	working dresses
		Mrs Washington	
		Miss Millichip	typical maid's uniforms
Christina Lucy Vergette	crinoline gown	Jenny and Kitty	
Lady Harriet F. Osbourne	bustle gown with apron-front	Daisy	
Mrs Andrew Carlisle		Lady Pandora L. Vergette	Victorian party dress
Lady Victoria A. Vergette	bustle gown with divided front-skirt	Camilla R. Fitzroy	yoked Victorian party dress
Captain Charles Moffat	military uniforms	Miss Verity P. Carlisle	yoked dress with contrasting yoke
Colonel Edward J. Osbourne			
Commodore Andrew Carlisle	naval uniform	Venetia Wallis	pretty floral dresses with broderie anglaise pinafore
George Henry Vergette	formal suit with frock coat	Claire Nicholson-Walker	
William Edward Vergette	formal suit with morning coat		
		Lord Nicholas W. Vergette	sailor suit
Mr Borthwick	butler's suit	Digby Spencer	Victorian boy's suit
Mr Groucutt	casual jacket with trousers/lounge suit	Richard W. Osbourne	Highland costume
		John T Osbourne	

dress, not only represents the change of status in becoming a wife but is also designed to act as a powerful object to bestow happiness. 'Something borrowed', often from the mother or best friend, is usually an item associated with happy and successful ventures and thus is hoped to bestow the fortune of good luck on the bride. And 'something blue' – this colour has symbolically come to represent purity and, by wearing it on her wedding day, the bride is illustrating her intention to remain faithful to her new husband. I think that the line *And a silver sixpence in her shoe* may have been added at a later date and is self-explanatory in that it wishes financial security in the future.

The Bride

Wardrobe

This comprises:

- pantaloons
- lace-trimmed petticoat with train
- flounced top skirt for dress with fishtail
- ruched overskirt with ribbon trim
- basque bodice
- headdress and veil
- bouquet of silk roses

Materials Required

- ivory-coloured silk, satin or taffeta material
- ivory-coloured lace edgings in ½in (12mm) width and 1¼in (30mm) width
- narrow ribbon in a choice of pale shade (I selected peach and cream)
- finest silk tulle for the veil
- tiny crystal beads for the buttons
- tiny pearls for the necklace

Pantaloons

This is a pattern that will fit all female adult figures. It is a personal choice whether the garment is made in soft silks and satin or in crisp, white, cotton fabric. For the bride I used the same soft ivory satin for all garments.

1. Cut out the pattern on double fabric and transfer all the markings on to the fabric.
2. Pin and stitch the front seam A–B.
3. Attach narrow lace ½in (12mm) to the leg hems and leave enough thread at each end to gather when fitted on to the doll.
4. Turn and stitch a ¼in (6mm) hem at the waist and again leave thread at each end to gather.
5. Pin and stitch the back seam C–D.
6. With the *right sides together* form the pantaloon shape; stitch the inside leg in one continuous operation.

7. Clip almost to the stitching line at the gusset before turning through to the right side and press.

8. Fit on to the doll and gather tightly into the waist and above each section of porcelain leg. Secure all threads and use to slip-stitch the lace edges on the hems.

Petticoat

1. Cut out the three pattern pieces and transfer all markings on to the fabric.

2. With the *right sides together* pin and stitch the front side seams A–B to the back side seams A–B.

3. Press flat and then attach ½in (12mm) lace along the hemline, leaving a slight overlap at point E. Press.

4. Using a large stitch, sew two rows across the waist-line and leave threads at each end to gather when fitted on to the doll.

5. Pin and stitch the back seam C–D. Leaving an opening 1¼in (30mm) at the waist, stitch through to the outer edge of lace trim.

6. Fit on to the doll and gather tightly into the waist; secure all threads.

Wedding-Dress Skirt

1. Cut out the three pattern pieces and transfer all markings on to the fabric. Cut a length of ivory satin 20in × 2in (51cm × 5cm) for the hemline flounce.

2. With the *right sides together* pin and stitch the front side seams A–B to the back side seams A–B. Press flat.

3. Turn a narrow hem along one 20in (51cm) edge of the base flounce and press.

4. Pin 1¼in (30mm) wide lace along the top edge of the flounce and, using a large stitch, sew two rows so that the fabric and lace will gather together.

5. Pin the centre point of the flounce to the centre front skirt at F and gather evenly from each end on to the lower edge of the prepared skirt.

6. Pin and stitch the back seam C–D. Leaving an opening 1¼in (30mm) at the waist, stitch through to the hemline of the satin flounce.

7. Fit on to the doll and gather tightly into the waist; secure all threads.

Fishtail

1. Cut out the pattern on double fabric. With the *right sides together* stitch round the edge leaving the top open. Clip the curve and turn through to the right side. Press. Stitch across the opening.

2. Cut three 5in (13cm) lengths of 1¼in (30mm) lace and gather on to the fishtail at the indicated levels.

3. Stitch narrow ribbon across the top of the fishtail such that a bow may be tied in the centre.

4. Slip-stitch the fishtail to the rear of the dress skirt, using the guideline indicated on the pattern.

Draped Overskirt

1. Cut out the quadrant pattern. Attach ½in (12mm) ivory lace round the curved edge.

2. Pull the two sides at points B and C, let point A fall to the rear and natural folds will begin to form. Pin these folds into place and adjust if necessary to even out. This process is made easier by working on an ironing board where pins can be pushed into the soft surface.

3. Using a large stitch, sew along the guidelines from the top fold to the edge of the lace trim. Secure the top threads and gather up tightly from the hemline to form the front drape. Secure all threads and attach small bows at these two points.

4. Place the drape over the dress skirt and pull the points to the back such that the gathers are in line with the side seams.

5. Overlap the lace at the top of the back seam and slip-stitch for 1¼in (30mm). Decorate with small bows.

Basque Bodice

Prepare the fabric by bonding on to lightweight Vilene or similar. This prevents the fabric from fraying since there are no turns or hems on this garment.

1. Cut out the pattern pieces and transfer all the markings on to the fabric.

2. If necessary, decorate the front bodice either with machine fancy stitches or by hand.

3. With the *right sides together* pin and stitch the front bodice to the back bodice pieces at the shoulders. Lay flat and press.

4. Stitch a row of gathering across the top of the sleeves ready to gather on to the bodice.

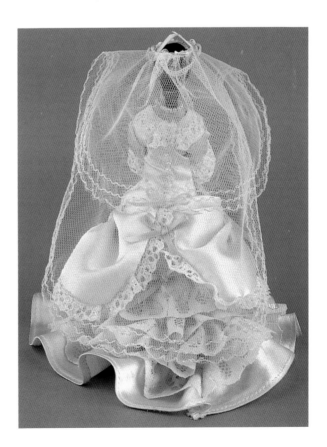

Bridal gown, rear view.

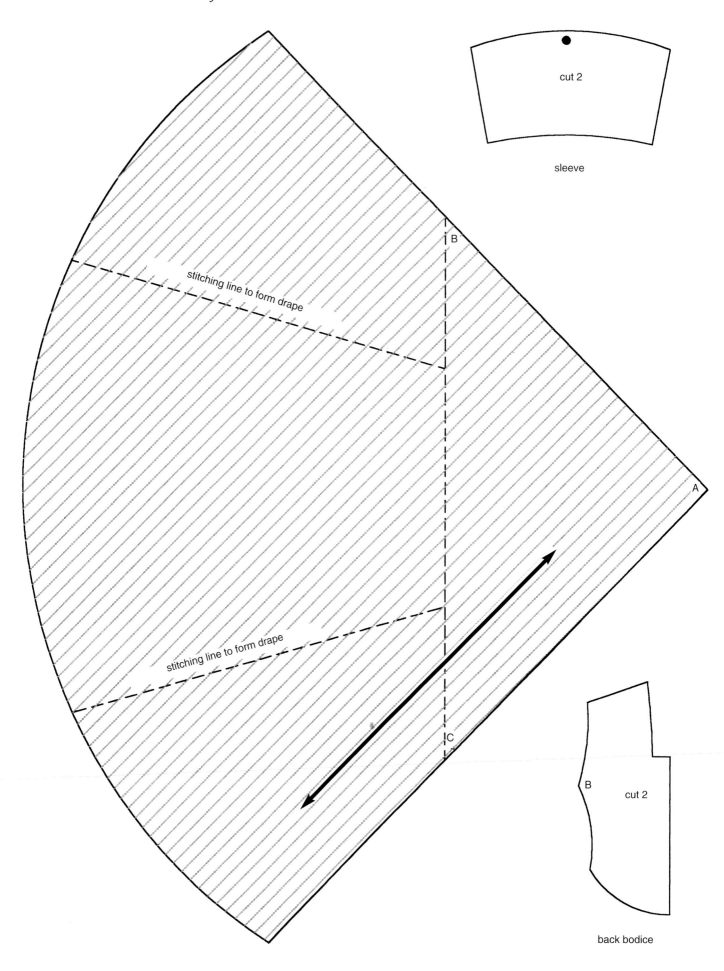

cut 2

sleeve

B

stitching line to form drape

stitching line to form drape

A

C

B

cut 2

back bodice

Bride's gown – pleated overskirt.

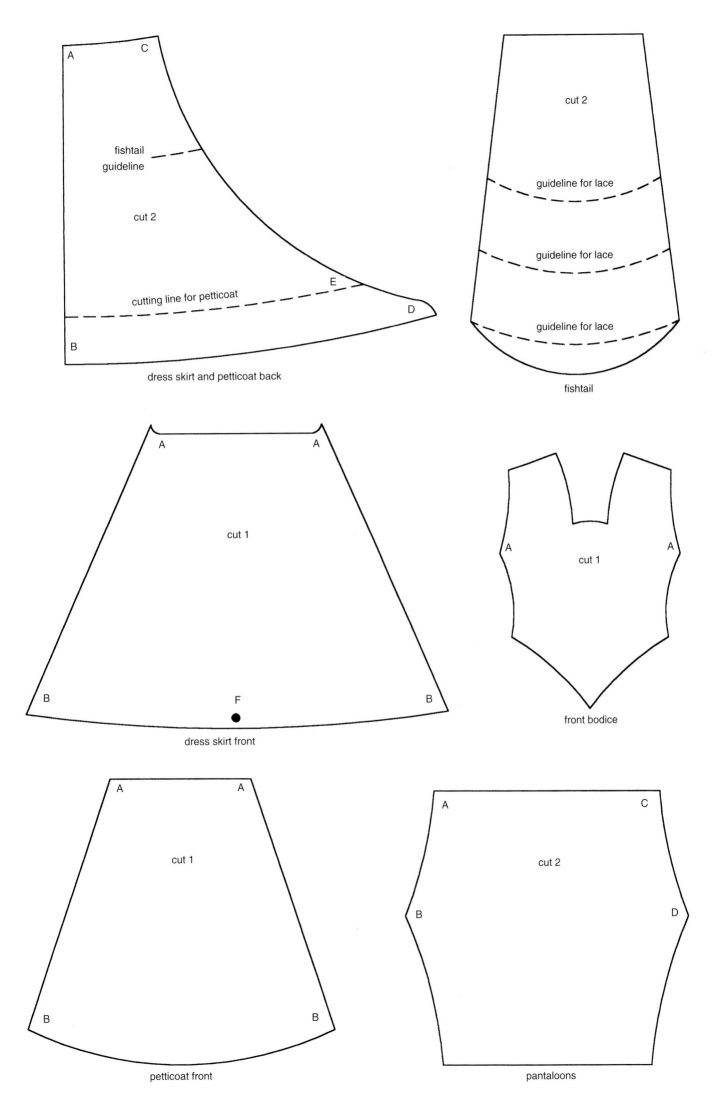

A

C

fishtail
guideline

cut 2

cutting line for petticoat

E

D

B

dress skirt and petticoat back

cut 2

guideline for lace

guideline for lace

guideline for lace

fishtail

A

A

cut 1

B

F

B

dress skirt front

A

A

cut 1

front bodice

A

A

cut 1

B

B

petticoat front

A

C

cut 2

B

D

pantaloons

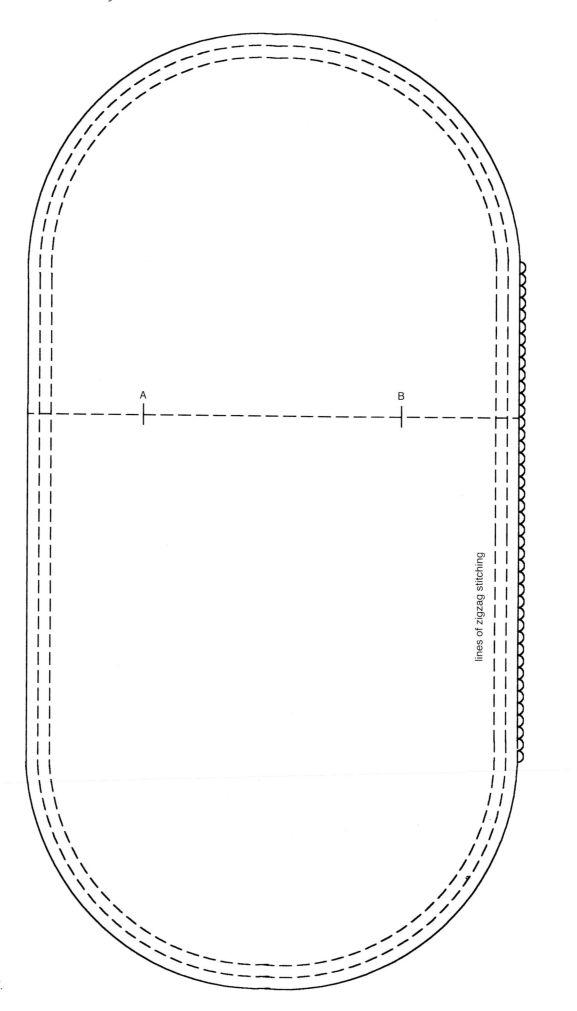

A   B

lines of zigzag stitching

Bride's veil.

5. Attach two lengths of ½in (12mm) lace to the cuff edge of the sleeves, leaving enough thread at each end to gather.
6. Matching the centre top of the sleeves to the shoulder seams, ease the fullness between A and B. Pin and stitch.
7. With the *right sides together* form the bodice shape and stitch the side and sleeve seams in one continuous operation. Clip almost to the stitching line at the underarm before turning through to the right side and press.
8. Use a strip of bias-cut bodice fabric to bind the lower edge of the basque.
9. Fit on to the doll and slip-stitch the back centre seam.
10. Use a length of ½in (12mm) lace to create a collar and carefully glue into position.
11. Complete with crystal beads to represent buttons down centre back.

Veil and Headband

The veil and the headband are made separately and then combined to make the headdress. A simple way to construct a rosebud headband is as follows:

1. Tie double knots into a length of narrow ribbon

and secure the centre of each, with a single stitch to set their positions.
2. Arrange and glue small V-shapes of green ribbon between each bud to represent the leaves.

The veil is made as follows:

1. Cut out the veil using fine tulle; this will be more expensive than the normal coarse tulle available but the effect is more in keeping with ¹⁄₁₂ scale and worth the increased cost.
2. If shell edging is available on your sewing machine this will give a totally professional effect to the veil.
3. Create a decorative border by using the zigzag stitch round the circumference of the veil two or three times. Start ⅛in (3mm) from the edge and with each row ⅛in (3mm) apart.
4. If a sewing machine is not available I would advise that the edge be left untouched. However, here is an opportunity for some simple hand embroidery, using a fine thread to work a decorative border.
5. Using a gathering stitch, sew from A to B. Secure thread at A. Fold the shorter section of the veil on top of the longer section.
6. Gather tightly from B and attach the veil to the rear of the headband between the rosebuds.

The Maid of Honour

This consists of a crinoline gown. This beautiful gown is quite easy to construct and, by incorporating the flounce detail, the result produces the 'waterfall' illusion to the floor. It is further elaborated with the simple use of ribbon and lace, both 1¼in (30mm) wide.

Wardrobe

This comprises:

- pantaloons
- three-tiered petticoat with double lower and middle tiers of tulle
- bodice
- crinoline skirt

Materials Required

- peach-coloured (or other pastel shade) silk, satin or taffeta
- fine tulle as used for the veil of the bride
- tiny crystal beads to represent buttons
- tiny pearls for necklace
- ½in (12mm) ribbons for decorative detail
- 1¼in (30mm) ribbon and lace
- ⅛in (3mm) peach satin ribbon

Pantaloons

The pattern and instructions for making this garment are to be found in the bride's pattern.

Three-Tiered Petticoat

This petticoat is constructed in two layers and three tiers. The garment comprises three lengths of the fabric and two lengths of tulle to overlay the lower and the middle tier.

1. Cut the tiers in the following lengths: top tier at 6in × 1¼in (15cm × 3cm); middle tier at 9in × 1½in (23cm × 4cm); lower tier at 12in × 1½in (30cm × 4cm).
2. Attach narrow lace to one long edge of the lower tier; this forms the hemline of the garment. Using a large stitch, sew across the top of the tier in readiness to gather.
3. Pin the centre of the lower tier to the centre of the middle tier and gather evenly from both ends towards the centre. Pin and stitch.
4. Repeat stages 2 and 3 with the two tulle tiers.
5. Place the tulle over the main fabric and stitch through total thickness across the raw edges ready to gather on to the top tier.
6. This double layer is gathered in a single operation on to the top tier.
7. There are now two back seams to be stitched: the two lower tulle tiers and the complete seam from waist to hemline on the main fabric.

8. Fit the petticoat on to the doll and gather tightly into the waist before securing all threads.

Dress Skirt

For this dress I recommend the use of ribbon and lace in similar widths of 1¼in (30mm), since equal lengths of both will form each flounce with no necessity for hemming. A toning shade in either satin or taffeta will be required for the bodice and for the insertion strips used to construct the crinoline skirt.

The insertion pieces of fabric that join the flounces are each 1½in (40mm) in width, this allows for two

¼in (6mm) seams, both top and bottom, resulting in the flounces overlapping to give the 'waterfall' illusion.

1. Cut out the dress skirt top on double fabric. Pin and stitch the short sides.
2. Cut the flounces in the following lengths: top flounce at 9in (23cm); central flounce at 12in (30cm); and lower flounce at 18in (46cm).
3. Pin and stitch the short sides of each flounce to form three circles.
4. Cut two strips of fabric at 12in × 1¼in (30cm × 3cm) and 9in × 1¼in (23cm × 3cm). Pin and stitch the short sides to form two circles.
5. Gather the lower flounce on to the lower edge of the 12in (30cm) circle. Pin and stitch.

6. Pin the central flounce round the top of the 12in (30cm) circle and stitch through total thickness ready to gather.
7. Gather the central flounce on to the lower edge of the 9in (23cm) circle. Pin and stitch.
8. Pin the top flounce round the top of the 9in (23cm) circle and stitch through total thickness ready to gather.
9. Gather the top flounce on to the dress skirt top. Pin and stitch.
10. Using a large stitch, sew two rows round the waist and fit on to the doll. Gather tightly and secure the threads.

Basque Bodice

The fabric should be prepared by bonding on to light-weight Vilene or something similar. This prevents the fabric from fraying since there are no turns or hems on the garment.

1. Cut out the pattern pieces, or, for extra precision, draw round the pattern on the reverse side of the fabric and then cut out.

2. With the *right sides together* pin and tack the shoulder seams before stitching. Press.
3. With the *right sides together* pin and tack the side seams before stitching.
4. Turn through to the right side and press lightly.
5. Fit on to the doll and slip-stitch the centre back seam closed.
6. Finish the raw sleeve edges and the bodice hem with a narrow matching or toning ribbon ⅛in (3mm).
7. Stitch tiny crystal beads to represent buttons down centre back seam.

Collar

The collar is formed from a 4in (10cm) length of scalloped lace, as used for the dress skirt.
1. Gather up the lace between the two centre scallops to form the centre front collar.
2. Pin the centre front in place and fold the lace to the centre back, going round the top of the shoulders so that the collar stands up to frame the head and shoulders. Pin in position at top of each sleeve.
3. Slip-stitch the centre back seam and secure the collar with several stitches at each point where pinned.

place on fold

petticoat – top tier

place on fold

petticoat – middle tier

place on fold

petticoat – lower tier

The Maid of Honour.

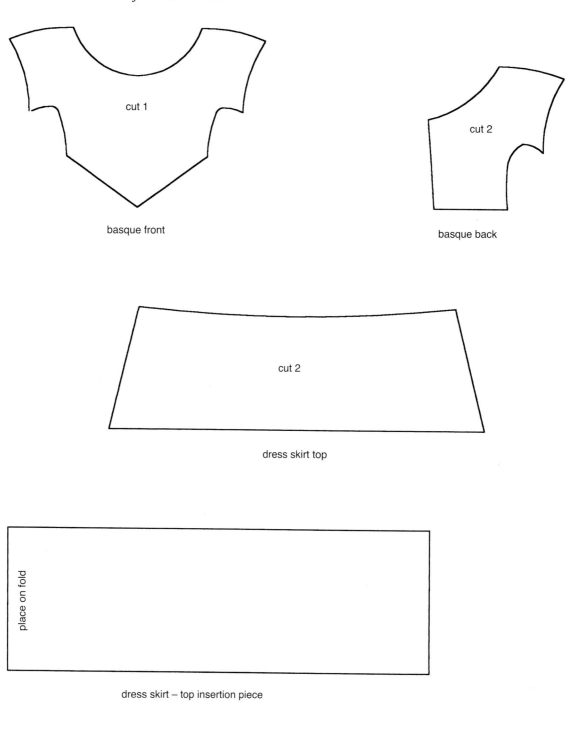

cut 1

basque front

cut 2

basque back

cut 2

dress skirt top

place on fold

dress skirt – top insertion piece

place on fold

dress skirt – lower insertion piece

The maid of honour.

The Marchioness

The mother of the bride wears a crinoline gown.

Wardrobe

This comprises:

- pantaloons
- three-tiered petticoat with double lower and middle tiers
- bodice
- crinoline skirt with flounce and lace detail

Materials Required

- fine white cotton/silk
- cinnamon-coloured taffeta/silk
- peach lace in three widths: ½in (12mm), ¾in (20mm), 1¼in (30mm)
- narrow brown velvet ribbon: ⅛in (3mm)
- bugle beads for necklace and buttons

Pantaloons

The pattern and instructions for making this garment are to be found in the bride's pattern.

Three-Tiered Petticoat

It was quite normal for as many as six petticoats to be worn to hold out the bell-shaped skirt of the crinoline gown. However, I found that this petticoat, with two middle and two lower tiers together with a single top tier gathered into the waist, was adequate to give the same effect. You may add a further middle and lower tier, giving the effect of three petticoats, but any more becomes cumbersome.

1. Cut the tiers in the following lengths: top tier at 6in × 1¼in (15cm × 3cm); cut two middle tiers at 9in × 1½in (23cm × 4cm); and cut two lower tiers at 12in × 1½in (30cm × 4cm).
2. Attach ½in (6mm) lace to one long edge of each lower tier to form the hemline of the garment.
3. Using a large stitch, sew across the top edge of each lower tier in readiness to gather.
4. Pin the centre of one lower tier to the centre of one middle tier and gather evenly from both ends towards the centre. Pin and stitch.
5. Repeat step 4 with the second lower tier and the second middle tier.
6. Place the above sections one on top of the other and pin together the two long raw edges. Then stitch through the double thickness ready to gather the two layers in one operation on to the top tier.
7. Pin the centre of the middle tier to the centre of the top tier and gather evenly from both ends towards the centre. Pin and stitch.
8. Using a large stitch, sew two rows of gathering across the waistline ready to fit on to the doll.
9. With the *right sides together* pin and stitch the centre back seam from waist to hemline (check that the inner middle and lower tiers are not caught into this seam).
10. With the *right sides together* pin and stitch the centre back seam of the inner middle and the lower tier.
11. Fit the petticoat on to the doll and gather tightly into the waist.

Bodice

1. Cut out the bodice pattern pieces on double fabric: two front bodice, four back bodice, and transfer all the markings on to the fabric.
2. Cut out two sleeves and two cuffs and transfer any markings on to the fabric.
3. This is a basic bodice and so follow the instructions as given in Chapter 7. Before beginning construction decorate one front bodice with a V-shape of lace so that all the raw edges will be stitched into the shoulder seams.

4. Stitch across the top of the sleeves and across their lower edges and leave thread to gather at each end.
5. With the *right sides together* stitch the two side seams on each cuff. Turn through to the right side and press. It is helpful to stitch across the raw edges.
6. With the *right sides together* gather the lower edge of each sleeve on to a cuff. Pin and stitch.
7. Matching the centre top of the sleeves to the shoulder seams, ease the fullness between A and B. Pin and stitch.
8. With the *right sides together* form the bodice shape and stitch the side and sleeve seams in one continuous operation. Double stitch at the right angle underarm for strength and clip almost to point AB.
9. Turn the bodice through to the right side and press the side seams only.
10. Stitch a row of tiny beads (buttons) down the right back bodice and along each cuff.
11. Fit on to the doll and slip-stitch the centre back seam closed. Wrap each cuff as tightly as possible along the lower arm and slip-stitch into place.

Dress Skirt

1. Cut out the pattern pieces for the dress skirt and the flounce and transfer all markings on to the fabric.
2. Turn a narrow hem along one long edge of the flounce and, using a large stitch, sew across the opposite side, ready to gather on to the hem of the skirt.
3. Matching the centre of the flounce to the centre hemline of the skirt, gather evenly from both ends to the centre. Pin and stitch.
4. Take a 24in (61cm) length of 1¼in (30mm) wide peach lace and gather on to the skirt ½in (12mm) above the flounce.
5. Using a large stitch, sew two rows of gathering across the waistline ready to gather on to the waistband.
6. Cut the waistband 3in × 1in (75mm × 25mm). Fold in half lengthways and with the *right sides together* stitch across both short edges. Turn and press.
7. Matching the centre front skirt to the centre of the waistband, gather evenly from both ends. Pin and stitch. Press seam towards the hemline.
8. Matching the short sides of both the flounce and the lace, pin and stitch the back seam leaving an opening 1¼in (30mm) at the waist.
9. Stitch a length of narrow brown velvet ribbon along the gathering line of the lace flounce and finish with a small bow towards the front of the skirt.
10. Fit on to the doll and stitch the waistband to secure into place. Slip-stitch the back seam closed to complete.
11. The finishing touches may include a necklace and small coronet made from tiny crystal and pearl beads.

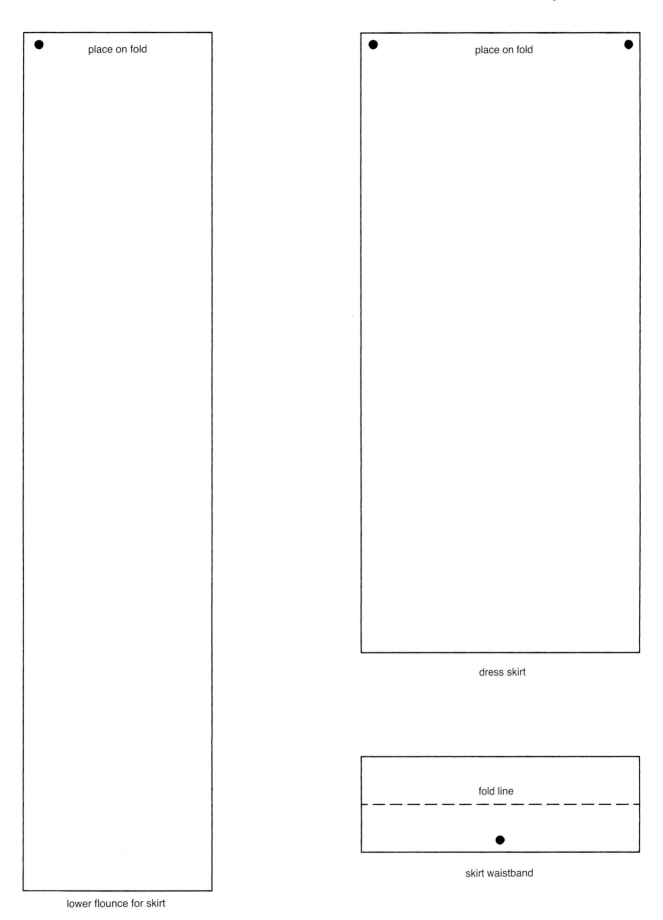

place on fold

place on fold

dress skirt

fold line

skirt waistband

lower flounce for skirt

The Marchioness, the bride's mother.

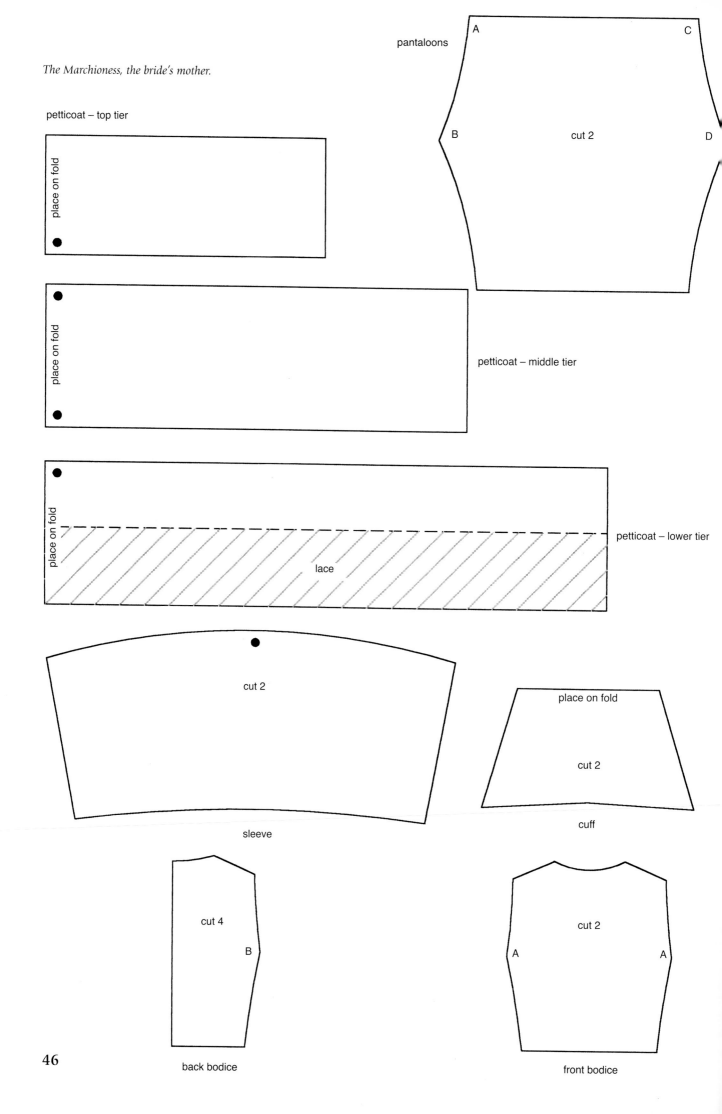

The Marchioness, the bride's mother.

pantaloons

A   C

B   cut 2   D

petticoat – top tier

place on fold

petticoat – middle tier

place on fold

place on fold

petticoat – lower tier

lace

place on fold

cut 2

sleeve

place on fold

cut 2

cuff

cut 4

B

cut 2

A   A

46

back bodice

front bodice

The Duchess

The grandmother of the bride wears a crinoline gown.

Wardrobe

This comprises:

- pantaloons
- three-tiered petticoat with double lower and middle tiers
- bodice with shawl collar
- crinoline skirt with pin-tuck detail
- small lace cap

Materials Required

- fine white cotton/silk
- grey taffeta/silk
- white lace in two widths: ½in (12mm) and ¾in (20mm)
- crystal beads for the 'diamond pin'
- bugle beads for buttons

Pantaloons

The pattern and instructions for making this garment are to be found in the bride's pattern.

Three-Tiered Petticoat

The pattern and instructions for this garment are as given in the Marchioness's pattern.

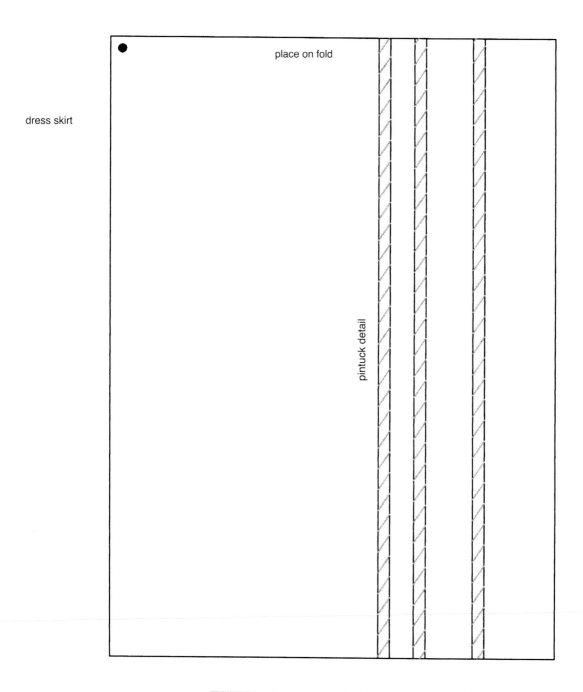

The Duchess.

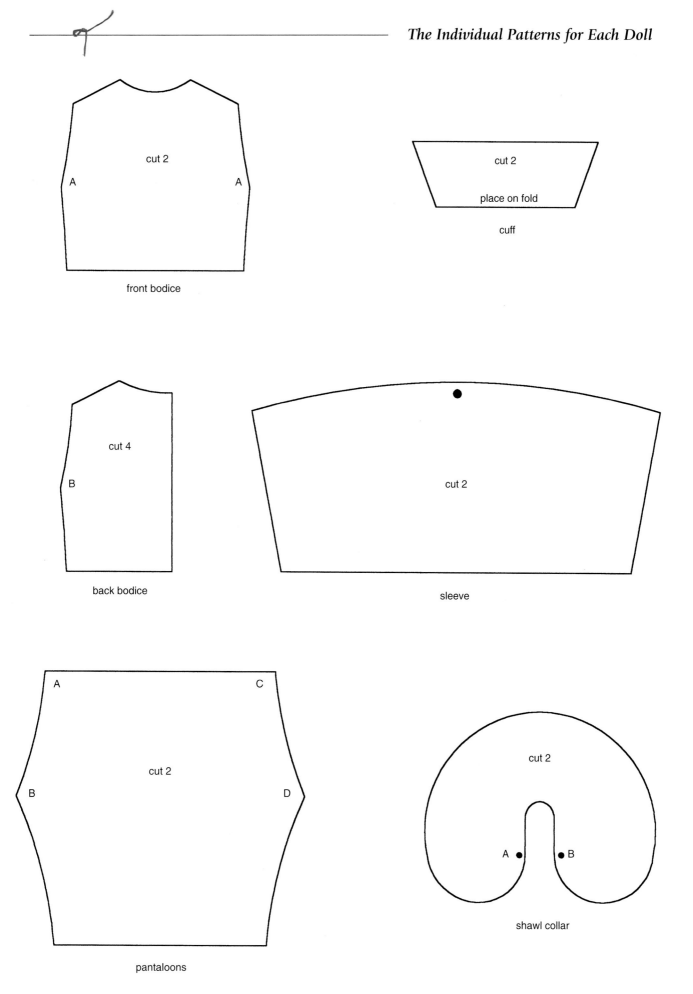

cut 2

front bodice

cut 2

place on fold

cuff

cut 4

B

back bodice

cut 2

sleeve

A   C

cut 2

B   D

pantaloons

cut 2

A   •   • B

shawl collar

The Duchess.

Bodice

1. Cut out the bodice pattern pieces on double fabric – two front bodice, four back bodice – and transfer all markings on to the fabric.
2. Cut out two sleeves and two cuffs and transfer any markings on to the fabric.
3. This is a basic bodice so follow the instructions given in Chapter 7.
4. Stitch across the top of the sleeves and leave threads to gather at each end.
5. Place the selvedge edge of white ¾in (20mm) lace along the cuff edge of the sleeves and tack into position. Using a large stitch, sew through the double thickness and leave threads to gather at each end.
6. With the *right sides together* stitch the two side seams on each cuff. Turn through to the right side and press. It is helpful to stitch across the raw edges.
7. Gather the lower edge of each sleeve on to a cuff. Pin and stitch. You will see the lace ruffle form at the wrist.
8. Matching the centre top of the sleeve to the shoulder seams, ease the fullness between A and B. Pin and stitch.
9. With the *right sides together* form the bodice shape and stitch the side and sleeve seams in one continuous operation. Double stitch at the right angle underarm for strength and clip almost to point AB.
10. Turn the bodice through to the right side and press the side seams only.
11. Stitch a row of tiny beads (buttons) down the right back bodice and along each cuff.
12. Fit on to the doll and slip-stitch the centre back seam closed. Wrap each cuff as tightly as possible along the lower arm and slip-stitch into place.

Dress Skirt

1. Cut out the pattern piece for the skirt and transfer all markings on to the fabric.

2. Turn a narrow hem along one 12in (30cm) edge of the skirt to form the hemline.
3. Stitch three ⅛in (3mm) pin tucks close to the hemline, but at varying distances apart.
4. Using a large stitch, sew two rows of gathering across the waistline and leave threads to gather on to the waistband.
5. Cut the waistband 3in × 1in (75mm × 25mm). Fold in half lengthways and with the *right sides together* stitch across both short sides. Turn and press.
6. Matching the centre front skirt to the centre of the waistband, gather evenly from both ends. Pin and stitch. Press seam towards the hemline.
7. With *right sides together* matching each pin-tuck, pin and stitch the centre back seam leaving an opening 1¼in (30mm) at the waist.
8. Fit on to the doll and stitch the waistband to secure into place. Slip-stitch the back seam closed to complete.

Shawl Collar

1. Cut out the collar on double fabric using a silk-type material and transfer all markings on to the fabric.
2. Gather lace from A–B on to the right side of one collar piece, going all round the collar edge, but excepting the section to fit around the neck. Put the straight edge of the lace to edge of the collar. Pin and stitch into place.
3. Place the second collar piece, right side down, enclosing the lace and tack all round the collar.
4. Stitch round the collar, leaving a small opening at the centre back so that the collar can be turned through to the right side. Press flat.
5. Slip-stitch the opening closed under the lace edge before placing on the doll and secure with a couple of stitches at centre front. Complete with a large Victorian-style brooch either in pearl, cameo or diamond.

Lady Harriet Francis Osbourne

She wears a bustle gown with an apron front.

Wardrobe

- pantaloons
- petticoat
- dress underskirt
- dress overskirt
- basque bodice

Materials Required

- fine white cotton/silk
- aubergine-coloured taffeta/silk
- white lace: 1¼in (30mm)
- ivory lace in two widths: ½in (12mm) and ¾in (20mm)
- narrow turquoise ribbon: ⅛in (3mm)
- beads for decoration and necklace

Pantaloons

The pattern and instructions for making this garment are to be found in the bride's pattern.

Petticoat

1. Cut out the three pattern pieces and transfer all markings on to the fabric.
2. With the *right sides together* pin and stitch the front side seams A–B to the back side seams A–B.
3. Press flat and then attach 1¼in (30mm) lace along the hemline, leaving a slight overlap at point E. Press.

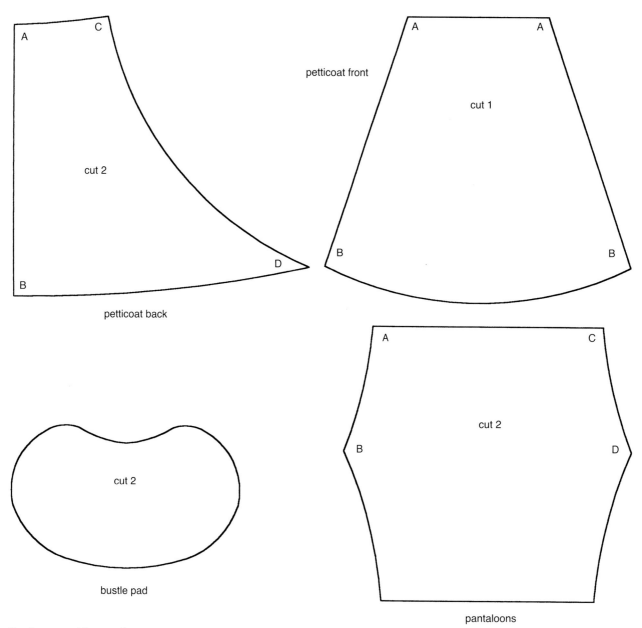

petticoat back

petticoat front

cut 1

cut 2

bustle pad

pantaloons

cut 2

Bustle gown with apron front.

4. Using a large stitch, sew two rows across the waist-line and leave threads at each end to gather when fitted on to the doll.
5. Pin and stitch the back seam C–D. Leaving an opening 1¼in (30mm) at the waist, stitch through to the outer edge of lace trim.
6. Fit on to the doll and gather tightly into the waist. Secure all threads.

Dress Underskirt

1. Cut out the three pattern pieces and transfer all markings on to the fabric.
2. With the *right sides together* pin and stitch the two front side seams G–H to the back side seams E–F. Lightly press the skirt open and flat.
3. Cut out the skirt flounce pattern and fold in half lengthways; the fold is the hemline of the skirt.
4. Using a large stitch, sew through the double thick-ness of the raw edges and leave threads to gather on

to the hemline of the skirt.
5. Decorate the flounce hemline with several overlap-ping layers of ½in (12mm) ivory lace.
6. With the *right sides together* and matching the cen-tre flounce to the centre front hemline of the skirt, gather evenly from both ends. Pin and stitch. Light-ly press along the seam towards the waistline.
7. Using a large stitch, sew two rows across the waistline and leave threads to gather when fitted on to the doll.
8. With the *right sides together* pin and stitch the back seam, inclusive of the flounce, leaving an opening 1¼in (30mm) at the waist.
9. Fit on to the doll and gather tightly into waist. Secure all threads and slip-stitch the opening closed to complete.

Dress Overskirt

1. Cut out the three pattern pieces and transfer all markings on to the fabric.

52

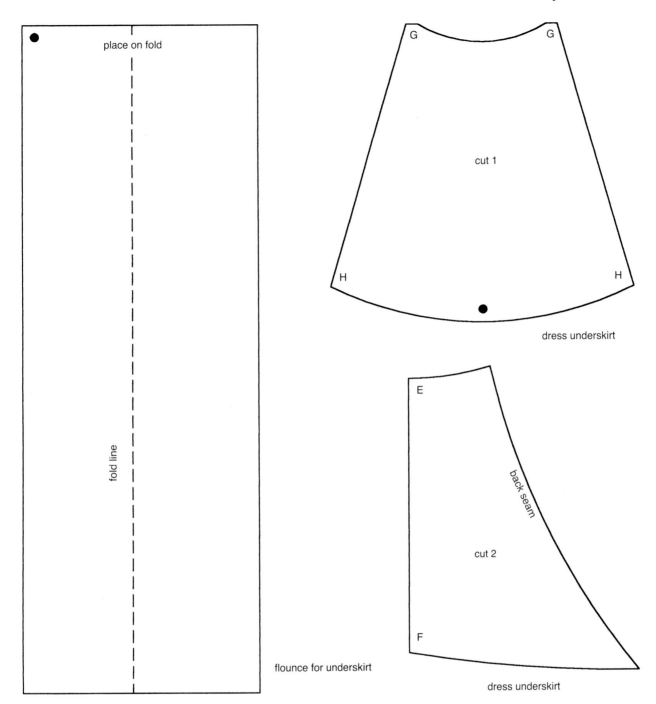

place on fold

fold line

cut 1

dress underskirt

flounce for underskirt

E

back seam

cut 2

F

dress underskirt

Bustle gown with apron front.

2. Mark with tailor tacking the two lines on the back pieces for the bustle gathers.
3. Pin and stitch the back seam A–B, leaving an opening 1¼in (30mm) at the waist.
4. Using a large stitch, sew the two parallel rows for the bustle gathers. Secure the threads at one end of each row and pull both pairs of remaining threads to the *right side* of the skirt to gather in the final stage.
5. With the *right sides together* pin and stitch one back side seam C–D to one front side seam E–F, using a large stitch. Secure threads at the hemline but leave threads at the waist to gather up the apron front at a later stage.
6. Repeat step 5 on the other side.

7. Using a large stitch, sew two rows across the waistline and leave threads to gather when fitted on to the doll.
8. Attach a slightly gathered ¾in (20mm) ivory lace frill round the hemline.
9. Gently gather the side seams at the waist to form the apron but retain threads in case any adjustment is needed. Fit on to the doll and gather into the waist, making sure the side seam threads are accessible. Secure and slip-stitch the opening closed.
10. Adjust the gathered sides so that the apron front is just above the flounce of the underskirt. Secure the threads with a few stitches at the waist.
11. Pin the underskirt and the overskirt at the side seams before gathering the two parallel rows to

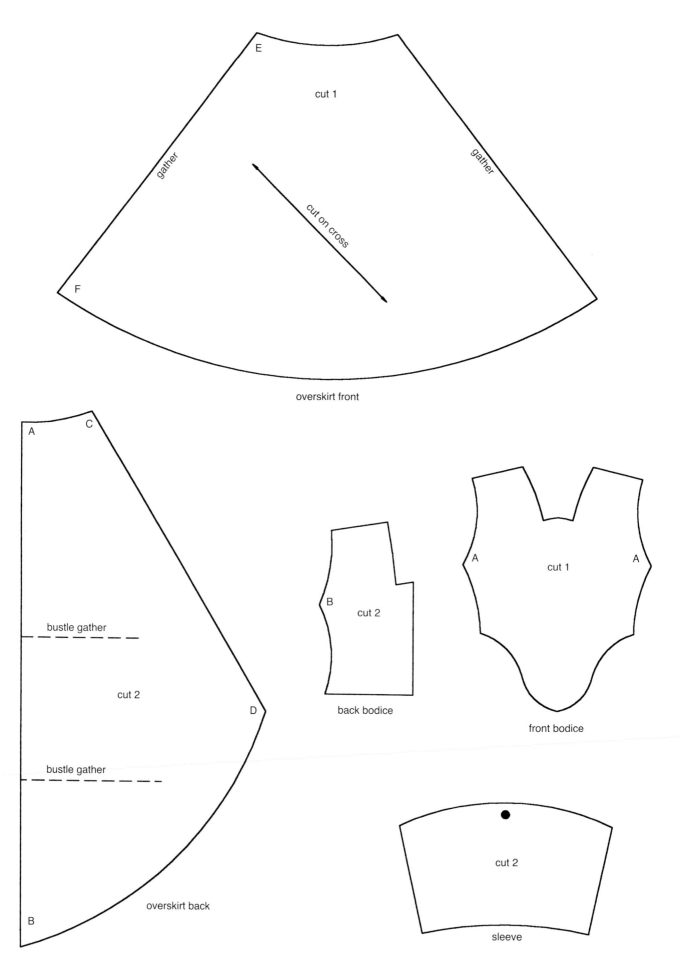

cut 1

gather

gather

cut on cross

overskirt front

A C

bustle gather

cut 2

bustle gather

B

overskirt back

D

B

cut 2

back bodice

A

cut 1

A

front bodice

cut 2

sleeve

Bustle gown with apron front.

form the bustle at the rear of the skirt. Secure all threads. Insert two bustle pads.

Bustle Pad

A simple but effective bustle pad may be made with mid-weight, non-iron Vilene or similar material. Cut out the pattern on double fabric and sandwich either a piece of wadding or cotton wool between the two pieces. Over-sew or overlock round the whole edge.

Basque Bodice

Prepare the fabric by bonding on to lightweight Vilene or similar sewing accessory.

1. Cut out the pattern pieces and transfer all markings on to the fabric.
2. If necessary, decorate the front bodice either with machine fancy stitches or by hand.
3. With the *right sides together* pin the front bodice to the back bodices at the shoulders and stitch. Lay flat, open the shoulder seams and press.
4. Stitch a row of gathering across the top of the sleeves ready to gather on to the bodice.
5. Attach ¾in (20mm) ivory lace along the cuff edges of the sleeves, leaving enough thread at each end to gather.
6. Matching the centre top of the sleeves to the shoulder seams, ease the fullness between A and B. Pin and stitch.
7. With the *right sides together* form the bodice shape and stitch the side and sleeve seams in one contin-

Bustle gown, rear view.

uous operation. Clip almost to the stitching line underarm before turning to the right side and press.
8. Use a length of bias-cut bodice fabric to bind the lower edge of the basque.
9. Fit on to the doll and slip-stitch the centre back seam.
10. Use a length of ¾in (20mm) lace to create a collar and carefully stitch or glue into position.
11. Complete with crystal beads to represent buttons down the centre back seam.

Lady Victoria Alice Vergette

She wears a bustle gown with divided front-skirt.

Wardrobe

- pantaloons
- petticoat
- dress underskirt
- dress overskirt
- basque bodice

Materials Required

- fine white cotton/silk
- emerald-green taffeta/silk
- ivory lace in three widths: ½in (12mm), ¾in (20mm) and 1in (25mm)
- narrow gold ribbon: ⅛in (3mm)
- a variety of beads for buttons and necklace

Use the garment patterns as given for Lady Francis Osbourne, except for the dress overskirt.

Dress Overskirt

1. Cut out the overskirt pattern and transfer all markings on to the fabric.
2. Mark with tailor tacking where the side seams will fall at A–B.
3. Mark with tailor tacking each end of the gathering lines that will form the bustle.
4. Using a large stitch, sew the gathering lines for the bustle. Secure all threads at one end of each line and leave the remaining threads to gather.
5. Gather 1in (25mm) wide lace round the outer edge of the overskirt from C–C. Press the resulting seam under the body of the skirt.
6. Using a large stitch, sew two rows across the waistline, including the lace edge at each end and leave threads to gather at a later stage.
7. Pin the overskirt on to the dress underskirt at centre back waist, side waist at A and lower side seam at B.
8. Gather tightly round the waist so that the lace edges meet at centre front. Secure threads.
9. Gather the two lines to form the bustle and secure the threads on the inside of the skirt.
10. Complete with small bows of golden ribbon and insert two bustle pads.

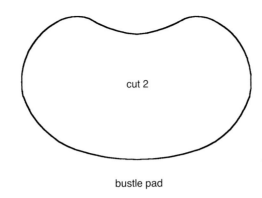

cut 2

bustle pad

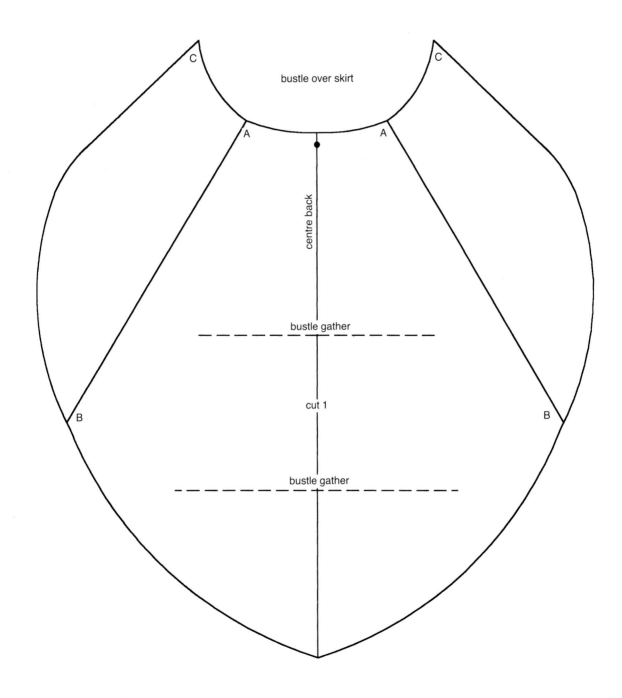

C   bustle over skirt   C

A   A

centre back

bustle gather

cut 1

B   B

bustle gather

LEFT: *Lady Victoria Alice Vergette.*
ABOVE: *Bustle gown with divided front.*

The Duke, the Marquis and Other Male Guests

Each wears the formal suit comprising either frock coat and trousers, or morning coat and trousers.

It is my opinion that the creation of a male jacket/coat is the most difficult garment to produce in miniature. For this reason I spent many hours practising on fine cotton toile before I was satisfied with the results from these pared-down patterns. All seams are reduced to ⅛in (3mm), removing any excess of fabric so that the seams will press sharply and the points of collars and revers are easier to tease out. To ensure a good, professional finish it is essential to press each seam open as it is sewn. I double stitch all curved seams for extra strength since these are clipped almost to the stitching line to give a good shape to the garment and for fitting purposes. I found it useful to take a needle with double thread and a single knot and from the inside of the garment push the needle into any point which you are turning through to the right side and to pull hard before cutting the thread. This has often given a crisper point than working with a pin to tease out the fabric.

With some of my dolls I persevered and used suiting worsteds, but it is a difficult fabric to work with as it has a tendency to fray easily. Cotton fabrics are easier to handle since the density of the weave means that they are slower to fray. I achieved an excellent result for the naval uniform with the use of cotton poplin. The pattern already allows for the skirt section of the jacket to be lined, but to give extra substance to the bodice I cut it out on bonded fabric, but I left the sleeves in non-bonded fabric to allow for natural creasing at the elbows.

If you are dressing the dolls for a child I would recommend the use of fine felt material as it is an easy medium to work with and can be purchased in a wide range of colours. The patterns would need some adjustment since the hems and some turnings would no longer be necessary. For example, I used the butler's jacket pattern to create the ceremonial costume worn by the groomsmen. Once I had traced and cut out the pattern pieces I shortened the sleeve by ⅛in (3mm) at the cuff, trimmed the same amount off the curved edges of the coat tails and trimmed the same again from the front edge of the jacket as facings were not necessary.

Wardrobe

- dress shirt
- formal suit
- waistcoat
- cravat or tie
- top hat

Materials Required

- fine white lawn
- fine worsteds or cotton fabric
- assortment of silk or taffeta for linings
- assortment of ½in (12mm) ribbons

Dress Shirt

Before cutting out any of the pattern stitch three to five pin tucks down the centre of a 3in (75mm) square of fine white lawn; use this for the shirtfront.

1. Cut out the pattern pieces, placing the centre front shirt on to the centre pin tuck. Note the collar is cut *on the cross* of the fabric. Transfer all marking on to the fabric with tailor tacking.
2. Complete the collar first since this is fitted on to the doll before the main bodice of the shirt. With the *right sides together* stitch the two sides. Turn and press.
3. Stitch lengthways across the centre of the collar, leaving thread at each end to secure under the chin of the doll.
4. Clip the raw edges several times before placing around the neck of the doll and secure in place by stitching tightly under the chin. Because the collar is cut *on the cross* it should lie neatly in position.
5. With the *right sides together* join the two shirt backs to the front shirt at the shoulder seams. Open and press.
6. With the *right sides together* stitch the two side seams on each cuff. Turn and press.
7. With the *right sides together* evenly gather each sleeve on to a cuff. Pin and stitch.
8. Matching the centre top of the sleeves to the shoulder seams, ease fabric between A and B. Pin and stitch.
9. Press the shirt before forming into shape, and with the *right sides together*, stitch the side and sleeve seams in one continuous operation.
10. Apply fray stop or similar to the neckline and the hemline.
11. Fit on to the doll, covering the raw edge of the collar and slip-stitch the centre back seam.
12. Secure the cuffs tightly into place by using tiny pearl or crystal beads as cufflinks.
13. Complete with a bow tie or a cravat. I use ¼in (6mm) ribbon to create a bow tie and ½in (12mm) ribbon for a cravat – this eliminates all raw edges which are not tucked out of sight.

Trousers

1. Cut out the pattern on double fabric and transfer all markings on to the fabric.
2. With the *right sides together* pin and stitch the front seam A–B, open and press.
3. Turn ¼in (6mm) hems at the waist and along the lower edge of each trouser leg. Tack, stitch and press. Alternatively, these hems may be bonded by using iron-on Vilene or similar.

4. Pin and stitch the back seam C–D. It is possible to adjust this seam slightly at a later stage to fit the waist.
5. With the *right sides together* form the trouser shape and stitch round the inside legs in one continuous operation. Double stitch in the gusset area for strength.
6. Clip almost to the stitching line at the gusset before turning through to the right side and press.
7. Fit on to the doll; if necessary adjust the back seam for a snug fit and secure with a few stitches at the waistline.

Waistcoat

This garment makes up simply by using a 9in (23cm) length of double-sided satin/silk ribbon, ½in (12mm) in width. Plain, striped or patterned ribbon may be used. It is entirely a matter of personal preference.

1. Fold the ribbon to form a V-shape with sides of equal length. Press.
2. Tuck the V point into the centre front of the trousers at the waist and secure with a few stitches.
3. Take the ribbon over each shoulder, cross at the back and tuck the raw ends into the back of the trousers at the waist. Secure with a few stitches.
4. Stitch four or five small matching beads down the centre front to represent buttons.

Frock Coat

1. Cut out the pattern pieces with great care. Cut the back neck facing and the coat skirt lining in black taffeta. Transfer all markings on to the fabric with tailor tacking.
2. With the *right sides together* join the two front coat to the back coat at the shoulder seams. Pin and stitch. Open the seams and press.
3. Turn ¼in (6mm) hems at the cuff edges. Stitch or bond into place. Press.
4. Matching the centre top of the sleeves to the shoulder seams, ease fullness between A and B. Pin and stitch.
5. With the *right sides together* form the coat shape and stitch the side and sleeve seams in one continuous operation. Double stitch underarm for strength before clipping almost to the stitching line. Turn through to the right side and press.
6. With the *right sides together* stitch the two sides of the collar. Turn and press.
7. Match the centre collar to the centre back neckline of the coat. Pin and secure in place.
8. Join the front facings to the back neck facing at the shoulder seams. Open the seams and press.
9. With the *right sides together* pin the coat facing to the coat from C–C. Match at rever points, shoulder seams and centre back neck before pinning the remainder in place. Note that the collar will be sandwiched between the coat and the coat facing.
10. Stitch from C, up the centre front, round the neckline, and down the centre front to C.

11. Clip round the neckline before turning the facing to the inside of the coat. Press the facing into the correct position and attach it to the seam allowance of the coat at the shoulder seams.
12. With the *right sides together* line the coat skirt. Clip the excess from the corners before turning through to the right side and press.
13. With the *right sides together* pin the centre back skirt to the centre back coat at the waistline, pin in both directions to the centre front. Stitch and press the waist seam towards the neckline.
14. Complete by using tiny beads to represent buttons, three or four on the *right* centre front and two at each cuff. Small corresponding stitches on the *left* front will represent the buttonholes.
15. Fit on to the doll; it may be necessary to hold the small revers in place with invisible stitches from the inside of the coat.

The Morning Coat

1. Cut out the pattern pieces with great care. Cut out the back neck facing only, in a toning taffeta. Transfer all markings on to the fabric with tailor tacking.
2. With the *right sides together* join the two front coat to the back coat at the shoulder seams. Pin and stitch. Open the seams and press.
3. Turn ¼in (6mm) hems at the cuff edges and stitch or bond into place. Press.
4. Matching the centre top of the sleeves to the shoulder seams, ease fullness between A and B. Pin and stitch.
5. With the *right sides together* form the coat shape and stitch the side and sleeve seams in one continuous operation. Double stitch underarm for strength before clipping almost to the stitching line. Turn through to the right side and press.
6. With the *right sides together* stitch the two sides of the collar. Turn and press.
7. Match the centre back collar to the centre back neckline of the coat, pin and secure into place.
8. Join the front facings to the back neck facing at the shoulder seams. Open the seams and press.
9. With the *right sides together* pin the coat facing to the coat, match centre back at the neckline, at the shoulders, at the rever points and continue down left and right fronts to the centre back of the coat. Seam the facing at the centre back hemline before stitching round the edge of the coat. Note that the collar will be sandwiched between the coat and coat facing.
10. Turn the facing to the inside of the coat and tack into place. Press the coat firmly.
11. Top stitch either by hand or machine before removing all tacking stitches. Give the coat a final press.
12. Complete by using tiny beads to represent buttons, three or four on the *right* side front and two at each cuff. Small corresponding stitches on the *left* front will represent the buttonholes.

The Duke.

The Marquis.

The Duke and Duchess.

The Marquis and Marchioness.

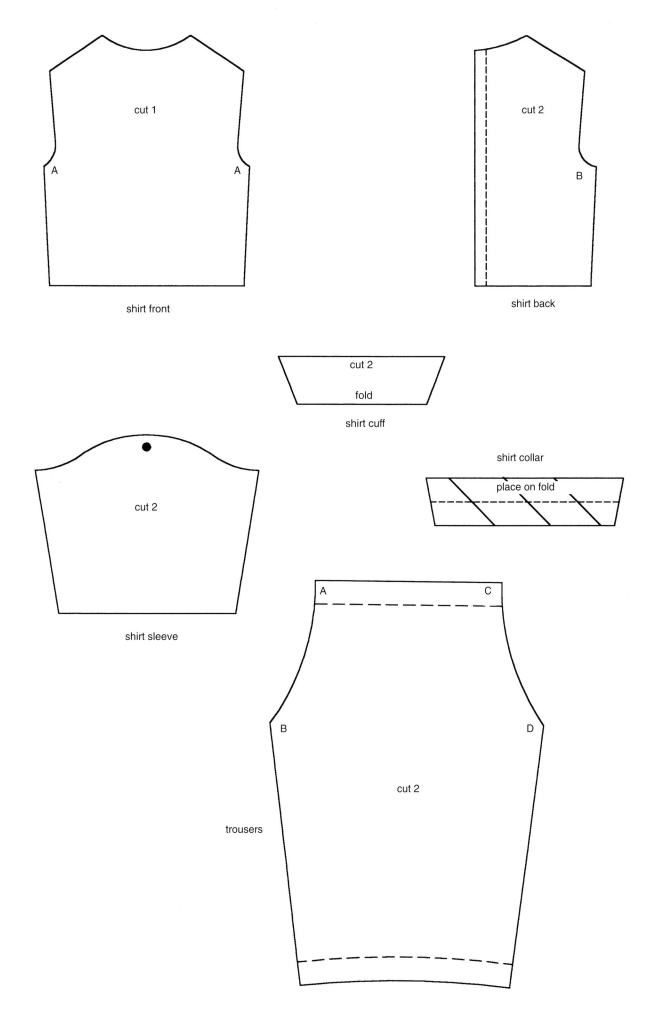

cut 1

A   A

shirt front

cut 2

B

shirt back

cut 2

fold

shirt cuff

shirt collar

place on fold

cut 2

shirt sleeve

A   C

B   D

cut 2

trousers

Dress shirt and formal suit trousers.

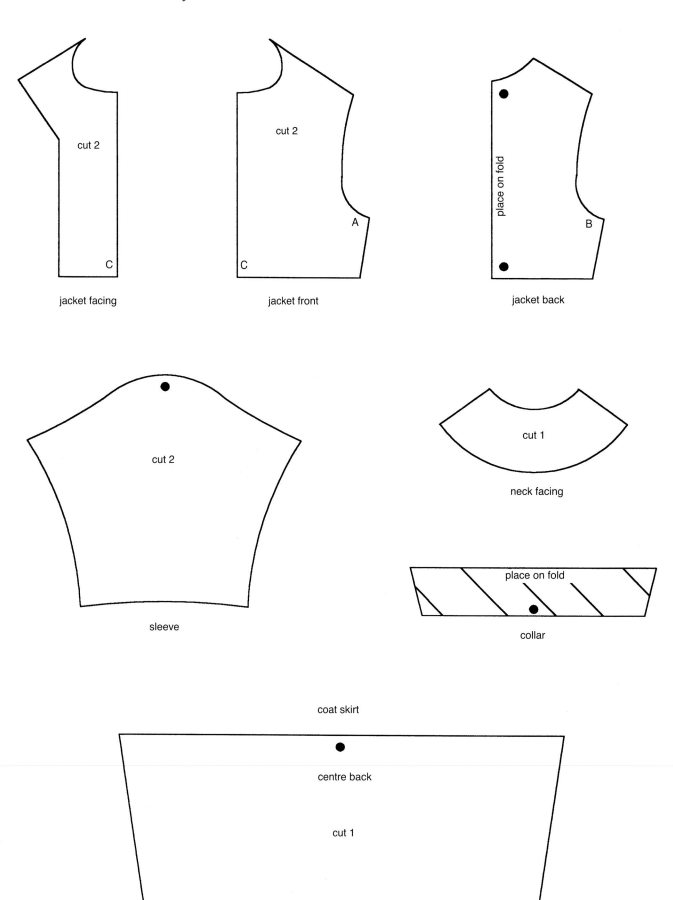

jacket facing

jacket front

jacket back

place on fold

cut 2

cut 2

cut 2

A

B

C

C

sleeve

cut 2

neck facing

cut 1

place on fold

collar

coat skirt

centre back

cut 1

Frock coat.

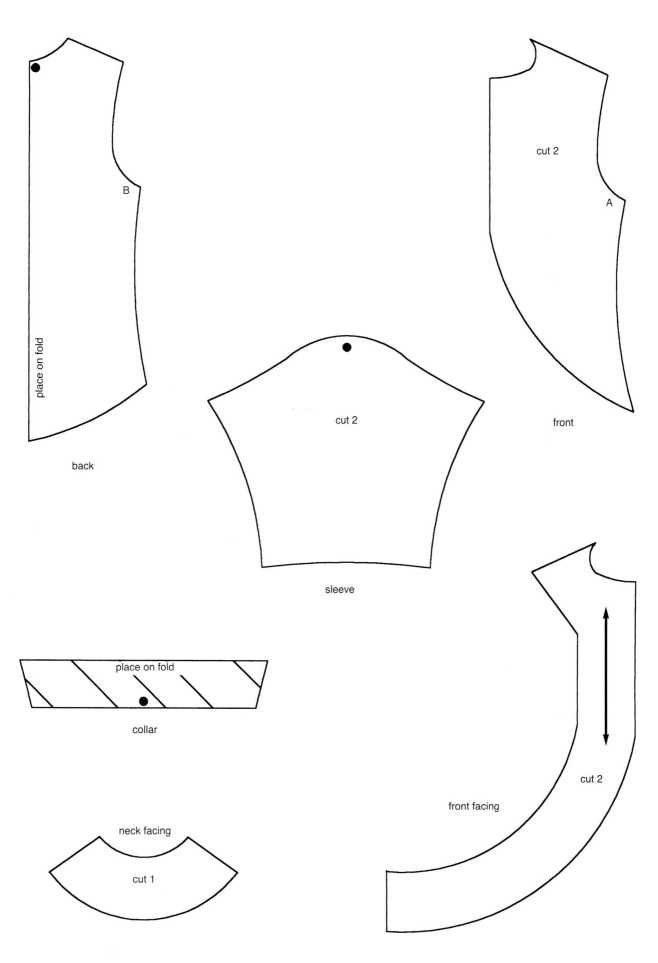

place on fold

B

cut 2

A

back

front

cut 2

sleeve

place on fold

collar

neck facing

cut 1

front facing

cut 2

Morning coat.

Captain Charles H. Moffat and Colonel Edward J. Osbourne

The military uniforms illustrated were inspired by my research at the Regimental Museum in York. Although it is impossible to produce all the original detail in miniature, I believe that it is possible to create acceptable illusions. The basic pattern is used for each uniform and only the decorative details differ:

The Princess Royal Dragoons, 1875–85.
The collar and cuffs are cream in colour with gold detail. The stripe to the side of the trousers is gold. Both the sash and the belt are gold in colour.

The Yorkshire Dragoons, 1880–85.
The collar and cuffs are black in colour with gold detail. The stripe to the trousers is gold. Both the sash and the belt are white leather.

The Royal Dragoon Guards, about 1886.
The collar and cuffs are black in colour with gold detail. The stripe to the side of the trouser is yellow. Both the sash and the belt are black leather.

I have included small pattern pieces for the collar, cuff and epaulettes, but you can cut these items freehand.

Materials Required

- scarlet red felt
- black felt or fine woollen crepe
- an assortment of golden braids
- oddments of leather (the best sources are gloves and handbags from charity shops)
- gold bugle beads for buttons

Trousers

1. Cut out the pattern on double fabric and transfer all markings on to the fabric. Fine black felt will not fray and does not need hemming: if using this material, adjust the pattern and omit hem allowance and the same at the waist. I opted to use a fine woollen fabric; this needs hemming.
2. Mark the centre of each trouser leg with a line of tacking stitches from waist to hem.
3. Stitch ⅛in (3mm) ribbon of the correct colour, centred along the marked lines.
4. With the *right sides together* pin and stitch the front seam A–B, open and press.
5. Turn a ¼in (6mm) hem at the waistline and along the hem of each trouser leg. Press.
6. Pin and stitch the back seam C–D.
7. With the *right sides together* form the trouser shape and stitch round the inside legs in one continuous operation. Double stitch in gusset area for strength and clip the curve.

8. Turn through to the right side and carefully press the inner leg seam; avoid creasing the outer sides of the trousers.
9. Lay the trousers with all seams meeting at the centre of trouser legs and press to form creases into the front and back.
10. Fit on to the doll and attach at the waist with a few stitches to avoid slipping.

Jacket

There is a ⅛in (3mm) seam allowance on the jacket made up in felt fabric (the distance from needle to the presser foot). All jackets and coats are worked so they can be laid flat on the working surface before the side and sleeve seams are stitched. When working with felt there will be no reference to right and reverse sides.

1. Cut out the bodice pattern pieces on fine red felt. Transfer any markings with tailor tacking.
2. Join the two front jacket to the back jacket at the shoulder seams. Pin and stitch. Open the seams and press.
3. Stitch a double row of stay stitches close to the neck edge to form a base for a stand-up collar.
4. Matching the centre top of the sleeves to the shoulder seams, ease fullness between A and B. Pin and stitch.
5. Fit the jacket on to the doll to check that the sleeve length is correct. Make any minor adjustments.
6. While the jacket can still be laid flat on the working surface, stitch on the buttons to ensure even spacing along a straight line. Use gold bugle beads and golden thread.
7. Form the jacket shape and stitch the side and sleeve seams in one continuous operation. Double stitch underarm for strength before clipping close to the stitching line. Turn through to the right side and lightly press into shape.
8. Cut out the collar and cuffs in the appropriate colour and glue into place on the jacket.
9. Decorate the collar and cuffs as illustrated with gold braid.
10. Fit the jacket on to the doll and slip-stitch the front edges together with a ¼in (6mm) overlap.
11. Cut out the belt and the sash from the appropriately coloured leather or other suitable fabric. Belt and sash are each ¼in (6mm) wide.
12. Form the epaulettes from gold braid, and glue or stitch into position.

Dress Items

You may wish to complete the doll in full ceremonial dress and, in order to do this, you will need to attach to the waist belt a narrow piece of matching fabric which is looped through the sword guard. Each end of the loop is inserted through a small slit in the waist belt and glued into position on the inside. The final addition to the doll is a ceremonial helmet that may be purchased from specialist sources.

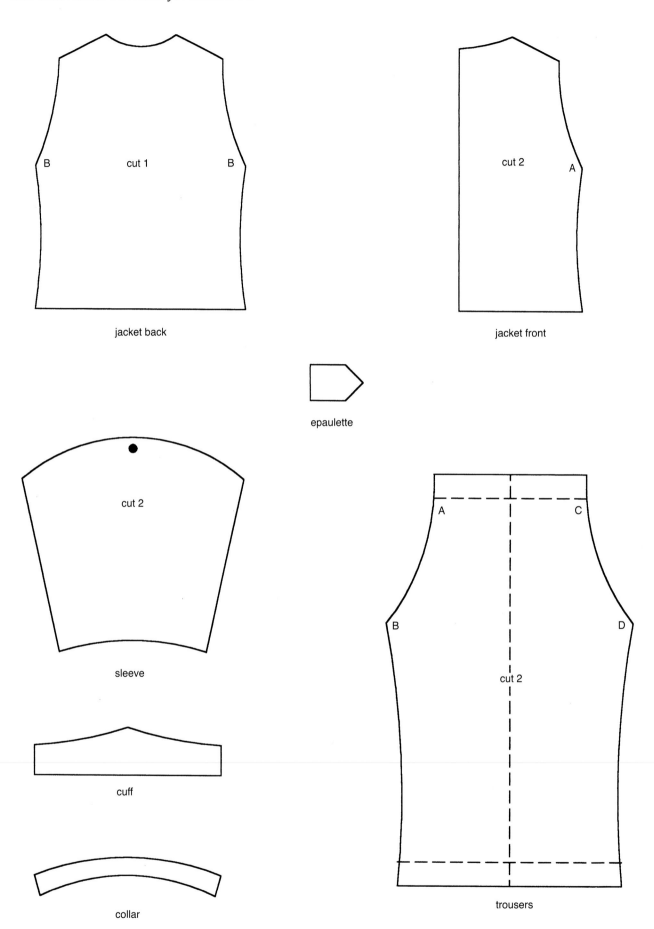

jacket back

cut 1

B   B

jacket front

cut 2

A

epaulette

cut 2

sleeve

cut 2

A   C

B   D

cuff

trousers

collar

Military uniform.

Commodore Andrew F. Carlisle

Materials Required

- fine white lawn
- navy blue cotton fabric
- ⅛in (3mm) black ribbon
- assorted golden braid
- gold bugle beads for buttons

Dress Shirt

Use the pattern and follow the instructions as given in the section on the formal suit. This is a plain-fronted shirt and so omit the pin tuck detail and cut out all the pattern pieces on plain white lawn.

Trousers

Use the pattern and follow the instructions as given for military uniforms; note that the ribbon detail is black.

Jacket

This jacket is an adaptation of the frock coat to present a double-breasted jacket with a shorter skirt.

1. Cut out the pattern pieces with great care and transfer all markings on to the fabric. Cut out the back neck facing and the skirt lining only in black/navy taffeta; transfer any marking on to the fabric.
2. With the *right sides together* join the two front jacket to the back jacket at the shoulder seams. Pin and stitch. Open the seams and press.
3. Turn ¼in (6mm) hems at the cuff edges and stitch into place. Press. On this garment do not take the option to bond the hems because of the braid and other details added to the cuffs at a later stage.
4. Matching the centre top of the sleeves to the shoulder seams, ease fullness between A and B. Pin and stitch.
5. With the *right sides together* stitch the two sides of the collar. Turn and press.
6. Match the centre back collar to the centre back neckline of the jacket. Pin and secure into place.
7. Attach the front facings to the back neck facing at the shoulder seams. Open the seams and press.
8. With the *right sides together* pin the jacket facing to the jacket from C–C. Match at the centre back neckline, shoulder seams and revers before pinning the remainder into place. Note that the collar will be sandwiched between the jacket and the jacket facing.
9. Stitch from C–C, up the centre front, round the neckline and down the centre front.
10. Clip round the neckline before turning the facing to the inside of the jacket. Tack and press firmly into position and attach to the seam allowance of the jacket at the shoulder seams.

11. With the *right sides together* form the jacket shape and stitch the side and sleeve seams in one continuous operation. Double stitch underarm for strength before clipping almost to the stitching line. Turn through to the right side and press the seams open. Insert a small roll of fabric into the sleeves to prevent creasing.
12. With the *right sides together* line the jacket skirt. Clip superfluous fabric from the corners before turning through to the right side and press.
13. With the *right sides together* pin the centre back skirt to the centre back waist; pin in both directions to the centre front. Stitch and press the seam towards the neckline.
14. Fit on to the doll to determine the point at which to fold back the revers. This is a double-breasted jacket and the fold will generally begin just above the top button so ensure that there is a sufficient gap between the waistline and the fold for either six or eight buttons. Pin the revers into place and remove the jacket from the doll.
15. Tack the revers into place and firmly press. Remove tacking only when the jacket is completed.
16. Stitch the buttons into place on the *left front* of the jacket.
17. Decorate the cuffs as illustrated with gold braid.
18. Fit the jacket on to the doll and slip-stitch the front opening closed.
19. Cut out a ¼in (6mm) wide belt from gold leather or other suitable material. If a miniature buckle cannot be obtained, fit on to the doll and join at the rear.

Dress Items

You may wish to complete the doll in full ceremonial dress; in order to do this attach a sword following the instruction given in the military uniform section.

Commodore Andrew Carlisle.

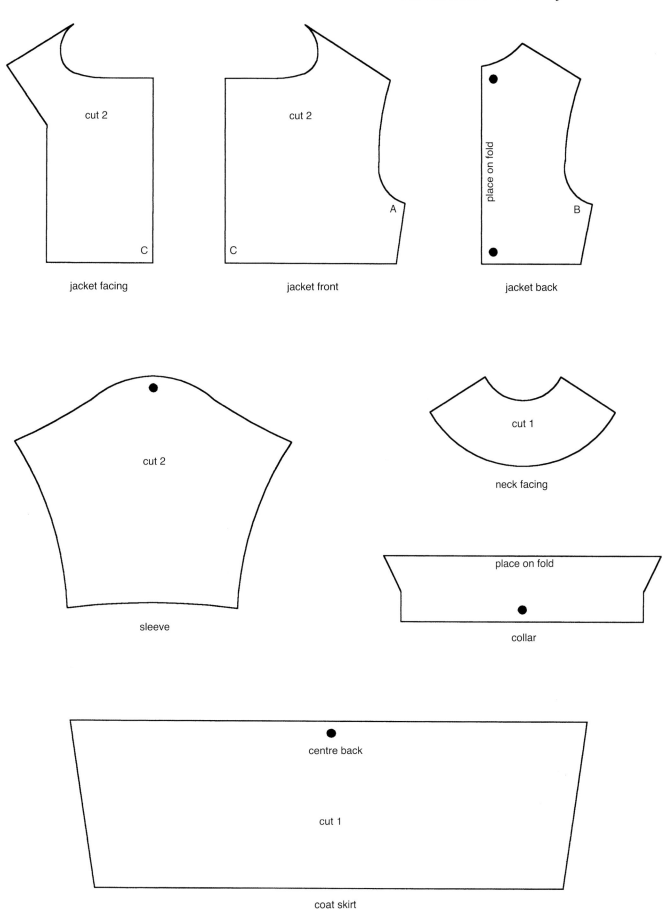

jacket facing

jacket front

jacket back

cut 2

cut 2

place on fold

A

B

C

C

cut 2

sleeve

cut 1

neck facing

place on fold

collar

centre back

cut 1

coat skirt

Naval uniform.

Mr Borthwick, the Butler

Wardrobe

- white shirt
- butler's suit
- colourful waistcoat
- black bow tie

Materials Required

- fine white lawn
- very fine black worsted or skirt-weight cotton fabric
- bright striped ½in (12mm) ribbon
- ¼in (6mm) black ribbon

Shirt

Use the pattern as given for the dress shirt in the formal suit pattern.

1. Cut out the pattern pieces, placing the centre front shirt on the centre pin tuck. Note that the collar is cut *on the cross* of the fabric. Transfer all markings on to the fabric with tailor tacking.
2. Complete the collar first as this is fitted on to the doll before the main body of the shirt. With the *right sides together* stitch the two sides. Turn and press.
3. Stitch lengthways across the centre of the collar, leaving thread at each end to secure under the chin of the doll.
4. Clip the raw edges several times before placing around the neck of the doll and secure in place by stitching tightly under the chin. Because the collar is cut *on the cross* it should lie neatly in position.
5. With the *right sides together* pin and stitch the two backs of the shirt to the front shirt at the shoulders. Open flat and press.
6. With the *right sides together* stitch the two side seams on each cuff. Turn and press.
7. With the *right sides together* evenly gather each sleeve on to a cuff. Pin and stitch.
8. Matching the centre top of the sleeves to the shoulder seams, ease fabric between A and B. Pin and stitch.
9. Press the shirt and, with the *right sides together*, form the shape and stitch the side and sleeve seams in one continuous operation.
10. Apply Fray Stop or similar to the neckline and the hemline.
11. Fit on to the doll, covering the raw edges of the collar and slip-stitch the centre back seam.
12. Secure the cuffs tightly into place by using tiny pearl or crystal beads as cufflinks.

Trousers

Use the pattern as given for the formal suit.

1. Cut out the pattern on double fabric. Transfer all markings with tailor tacking.
2. With the *right sides together* pin and stitch the front seam A–B. Open the seam and press.
3. Turn ¼in (6mm) hems at the waist and along the lower edge of each trouser leg. Tack, stitch and press. Alternatively, these hems may be bonded by using iron-on Vilene or similar.
4. Pin and stitch the back seam C–D. It is possible to adjust this seam slightly at a later stage to fit the waist.
5. With the *right sides together* form the trouser shape and stitch round the inside legs in one continuous operation. Double stitch in the gusset area for strength.
6. Clip almost to the stitching line at the gusset before turning through to the right side and press.
7. Fit on to the doll; if necessary adjust the back seam for a snug fit and secure with a few stitches at the waistline.

Butler's Jacket

1. Cut out the pattern pieces with great care. Cut the back neck facing and the 'tail' linings in black taffeta. Transfer all markings on to the fabric with tailor tacking.
2. With the *right sides together* join the two front jacket to the back jacket at the shoulder seams. Pin and stitch. Open the seams and press.
3. Turn ⅛in (3mm) hems at the cuff edges. Stitch or bond into place. Press.
4. Matching the centre top of the sleeves to the shoulder seams, ease fullness between A and B. Pin and stitch.
5. With the *right sides together* form the jacket shape and stitch the side and sleeve seams in one continuous operation. Double stitch underarm for strength before clipping almost to the stitching line. Turn through to the right side and press.
6. With the *right sides together* stitch the two sides of the collar. Turn and press.
7. Match the centre collar to the centre back neckline of the jacket, pin and secure in place.
8. Join the front facings to the back neck facing at the shoulder seams. Open the seams and press.
9. With the *right sides together* pin the jacket facing to the jacket from C–C. Match at rever points, shoulder seams and centre back neck before pinning the remainder into place. Note that the collar will be sandwiched between the jacket and the jacket facing.
10. Stitch from C–D, up the centre front, round the neckline, down the centre front and across to C.
11. Clip round the neckline before turning the facing to the inside of the jacket. Press the facing into the correct position and attach it to the seam allowance of the jacket at the shoulder seams.
12. Clip the seam allowance at C, on either side of the centre front ready to attach the 'tails'.

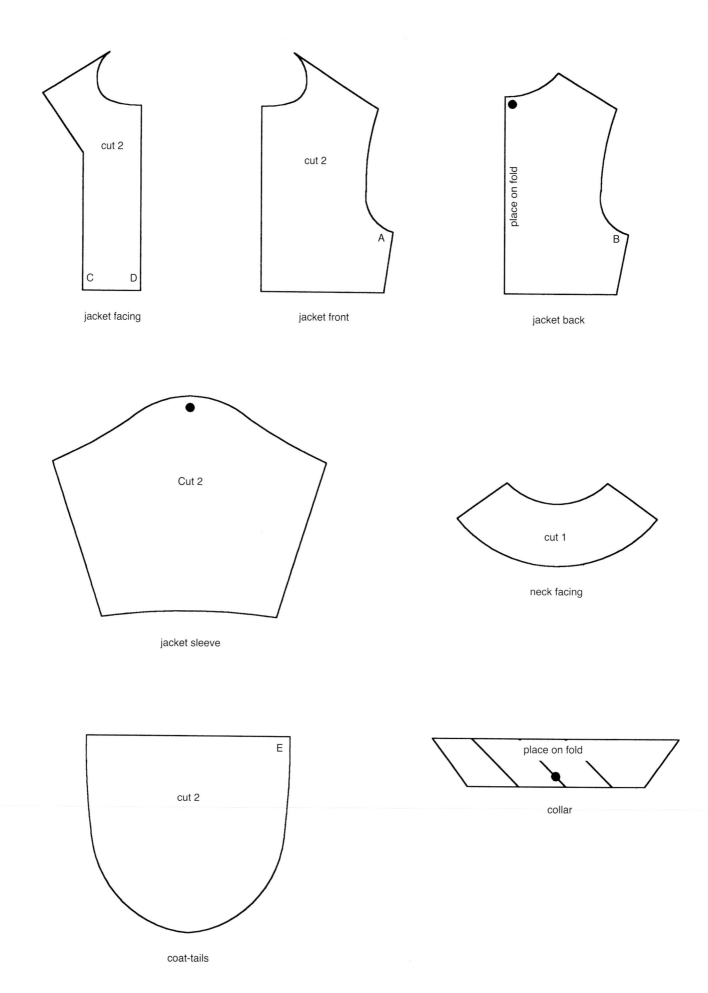

cut 2

jacket facing

cut 2

A

jacket front

place on fold

B

jacket back

Cut 2

jacket sleeve

cut 1

neck facing

C   D

E

cut 2

coat-tails

place on fold

collar

Butler's jacket.

13. With the *right sides together* line the two coat-tails, clip the curves, turn through to the right side and press.

14. With the *right sides together* pin one coat-tail at E to the side of C and continue to the centre back of the jacket. Repeat with the second 'tail' and the two will slightly overlap at the centre back. Stitch and press the waist seam towards the neckline.

15. Complete by using tiny black beads for buttons, three on the *right* centre front, two on each cuff and two at the centre back above the tails. Corresponding small stitches on the *left* centre front will represent buttonholes.

16. Fit on to the doll; it may be necessary to hold the small revers in place with invisible stitches from the inside of the jacket.

Waistcoat

This garment makes up simply by using a 9in (23cm) length of double-sided satin/silk ribbon, ½in (12mm) in width. Plain, striped or patterned ribbon may be used. It is a matter of personal preference.

1. Fold the ribbon to form a V-shape with sides of equal length. Press.
2. Tuck the V point into the centre front of the trousers at the waist and secure with a few stitches.
3. Take the ribbon over each shoulder, cross at the back and tuck the raw ends into the back of the trousers at the waist. Secure with a few stitches.
4. Stitch four or five small matching beads down the centre front to represent buttons.

Bow Tie

The tie is formed from ¼in (6mm) black satin ribbon and takes the form of a simple bow which is attached to the front of the collar.

Mr Groucutt, the Head Gardener

Wardrobe

- small-checked or striped shirt
- informal jacket
- trousers
- neckerchief

Materials Required

- brown/grey cotton fabric
- small-checked or striped cotton fabric
- brown check fabric
- ½in (12mm) green ribbon

Shirt

This is fitted on to the doll so that it opens down the front, allowing a neckerchief to be tucked into the open neck.

1. Cut out the pattern pieces and transfer all markings on to the fabric with tailor tacking.
2. With the *right sides together* pin and stitch the two front shirt pieces to the back shirt at the shoulder seams. Turn ⅛in (3mm) facings down each centre front and press.
3. On the collar turn ⅛in (3mm) hems along each long side and press. With the *right sides together* pin and stitch the two side seams. Turn through to the right side and press.
4. Matching collar centre to centre back shirt, attach by enclosing the raw edge of the shirt neck within the collar and stitch into position by hand.
5. With the *right sides together* pin and stitch the two side seams on each cuff. Turn and press.

6. With the *right sides together,* evenly gather each sleeve on to a cuff. Pin and stitch.
7. Matching the centre top of the sleeves to the shoulder seams, ease the fabric between A and B. Pin and stitch.
8. Press the shirt before folding into shape and with the *right sides together* stitch the side and sleeve seams in one continuous operation. Clip underarm before turning through to the right side.
9. Stitch buttons down the left front shirt and fit on to the doll, slip-stitch the front seam leaving the shirt open at the neck.
10. Secure the cuffs into place with gold bugle beads as cufflinks.
11. Place a silk neckerchief round the neck and tuck the ends inside the shirt.

Trousers

1. Cut out the pattern on double fabric and transfer all markings on to the fabric with tailor tacking.
2. With the *right sides together* pin and stitch the front seam A–B. Open the seam and press.
3. Turn ¼in (6mm) hems at the waist and along the lower edge of each trouser leg. Tack, stitch and press. Alternatively, these hems may be bonded.
4. Pin and stitch the back seam C–D.
5. With the *right sides together* form the trouser shape and stitch round the inside legs in one continuous operation. Double stitch in the gusset area for strength.
6. Clip almost to the stitching line at the gusset before turning through to the right side and press.
7. Fit on to the doll and secure with a few stitches at the waistline.

Casual Jacket

1. Cut out the pattern pieces and transfer all markings on to the fabric with tailor tacking.

Mr Groucutt, the head gardener.

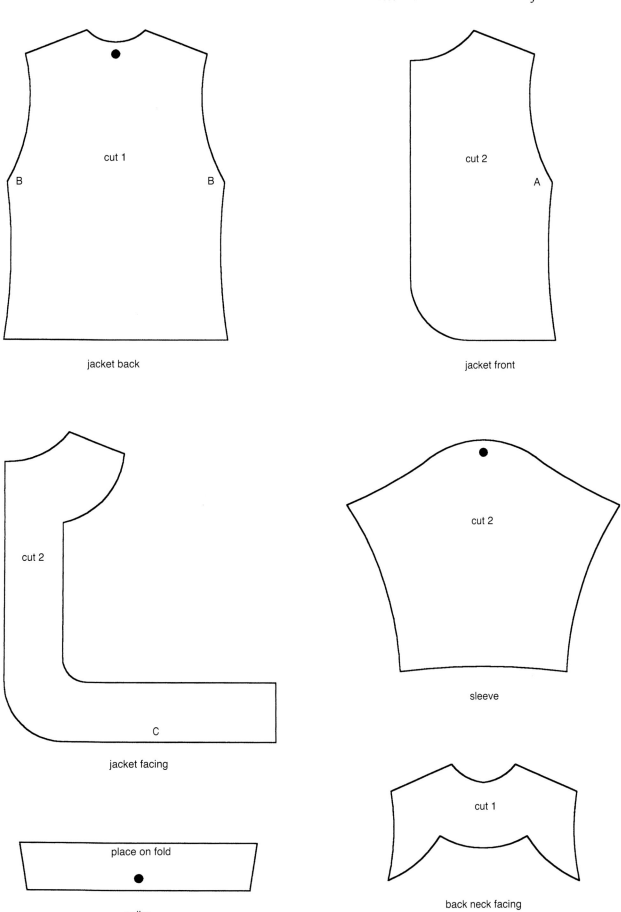

cut 1

B   B

jacket back

cut 2

A

jacket front

cut 2

jacket facing

C

cut 2

sleeve

place on fold

collar

cut 1

back neck facing

Informal jacket.

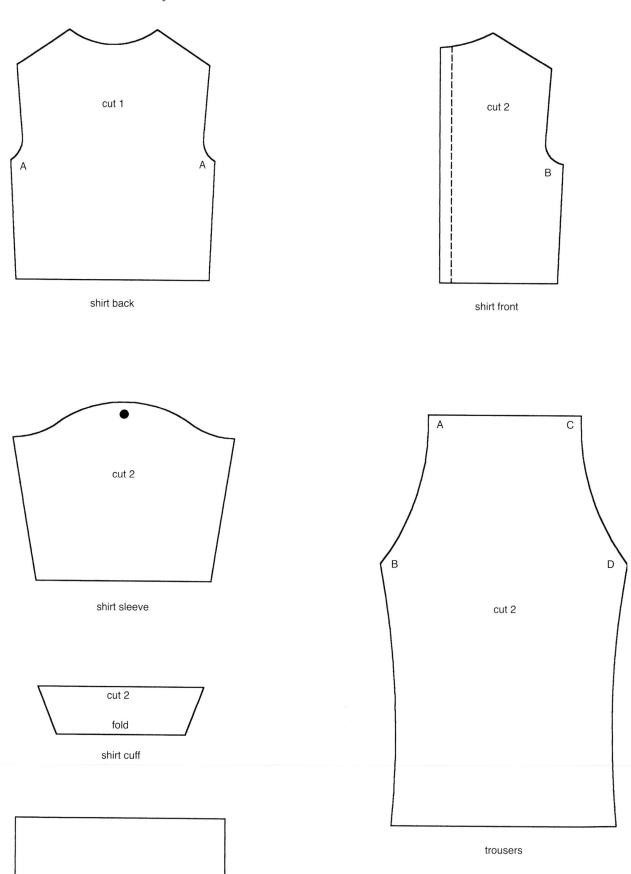

cut 1

A   A

shirt back

cut 2

B

shirt front

cut 2

shirt sleeve

cut 2

fold

shirt cuff

shirt collar

A   C

B   D

cut 2

trousers

Casual shirt and trousers.

2. With the *right sides together* join the two front jacket to the back jacket at the shoulder seams. Pin and stitch. Open the seams and press.
3. Turn ¼in (6mm) hems at the cuff edges. Tack, stitch and press.
4. Matching the centre top of the sleeves to the shoulder seams, ease fullness between A and B. Pin and stitch. Press.
5. With the *right sides together* form the jacket shape and stitch the side and sleeve seams in one continuous operation. Double stitch underarm for strength before clipping almost to the stitching line at A–B. Turn through to the right side and press.
6. With the *right sides together* stitch the two sides of the collar. Turn and press.
7. Match the centre collar to the centre back neckline of the jacket. Pin and secure into position.
8. Join the front facings to the back neck facing at the shoulder seams. Open the seams and press.

9. With the *right sides together* pin the jacket facing to the jacket, match centre back neckline at the shoulders, at the rever points and continue down each front to the centre back of the coat. Seam the facing at the centre back hemline before stitching round the edge of the coat. Note that the collar will be sandwiched between the coat and the coat facing.
10. Turn the facing to the inside of the coat and tack into place. Press the coat firmly.
11. Top stitch either by hand or machine before removing all tacking stitches. Give the coat a final press.
12. Complete with small beads to represent buttons, two at each cuff and three or four on the *right* side front; small corresponding stitches on the *left* front will represent buttonholes.

Waistcoat

Make up as for the butler's pattern.

The Groomsmen

Wardrobe

- ceremonial coat
- breeches
- hat and gloves

Materials Required

- felt fabric with choice of colour
- cream cotton fabric

Breeches

1. Cut out the pattern on double fabric and transfer all markings with tailor tacking.
2. With the *right sides together* pin and stitch the front seam A–B. Open and press.
3. Turn a ¼in (6mm) hem at the waist. Tack, stitch and press.
4. Pin and stitch the back seam C–D.
5. Run two rows of gathering across the hem of each breeches leg and leave thread at either end to gather.
6. With the *right sides together* form the breeches shape and stitch the inside leg in one continuous operation.
7. Clip almost to the stitching line at gusset before turning through to the right side and press.
8. Fit on to the doll and secure at waist with a few stitches. Gather tightly each breeches leg above the porcelain section. If possible, tuck the raw edges down into the legs.
9. From bonded fabric cut a strip ⅜in (9mm) wide to use for the knee cuffs. Alternatively, use a cream ribbon.
10. Glue the cuffs round the top of the porcelain legs, ensuring that they are in close contact with the breeches legs. Place the joins to the rear of the leg.
11. Complete with some detail on the outside edge of each cuff: buttons, bows or ribbon tabs.

Ceremonial Coat

The use of fine felt cloth dispenses with a *right* and a *reverse* side, therefore no reference will be made to '*right sides together*' throughout the making up.

1. Cut out the pattern pieces with great care and transfer all markings on to the fabric with tailor tacking.
2. Join the two front coat to the back coat at the shoulder seams. Pin and stitch. Open the seams and press.
3. Matching the centre top of the sleeves to the shoulder seams, ease fabric between A and B. Pin and stitch.
4. Form the bodice shape and stitch the side and sleeve seams in one continuous operation. Double stitch underarm for strength. Clip almost to the stitching line at A–B.
5. Open the side and sleeve seams and carefully press over a small roll of fabric. (Insert the roll into the sleeve for this operation.)
6. Turn through to the right side and lightly press.
7. To avoid bulk at the waistline, join the coat-tails to the bodice with a flat seam, that is, as on pyjamas.
8. Match C to E and continue round to the centre back coat overlapping the 'tail' for ⅛in (3mm) on to the bodice section. Tack into position. Repeat with the second 'tail'.
9. Secure the 'tails' in place with two rows of parallel stitching round the flat seam at the waistline.
10. Fit on to the doll and check that the sleeve length is correct and that the coat fronts meet at centre front (Chanel style).
11. Check the fit of the stand-up collar before applying fabric glue to the two rows of stay stitching and fitting into place.
12. Decorate as illustrated, lavishly with gold braids, epaulettes and gold bugle beads.

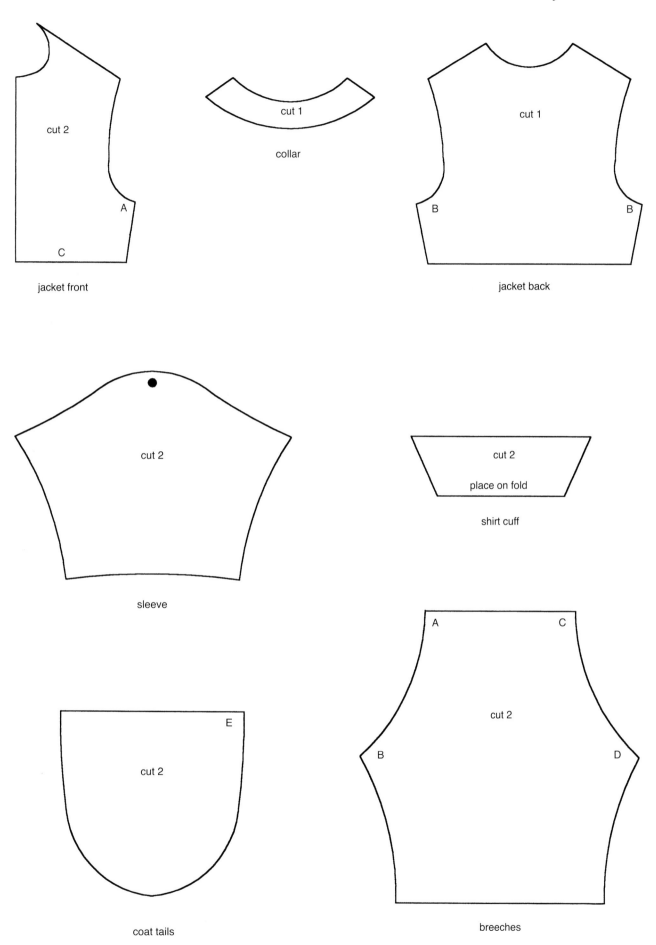

cut 2

jacket front

cut 1

collar

cut 1

jacket back

cut 2

sleeve

cut 2

place on fold

shirt cuff

cut 2

coat tails

cut 2

breeches

LEFT: *The groomsmen.*
ABOVE: *Ceremonial costume*

Mrs Drury, the Housekeeper

Wardrobe

- pantaloons
- petticoat
- bodice
- dress skirt
- apron

Materials Required

- white cotton fabric
- black silk/taffeta fabric
- ½in (12mm) wide white lace
- ¾in (20mm) wide white lace
- ¼in (6mm) wide white tape
- black bugle beads for buttons

Pantaloons

This is a pattern which will fit all the senior members of the household staff. I used a white cotton lawn for all the undergarments.

1. Cut out the pattern on double fabric and transfer all of the markings on to the fabric with tailor tacking.
2. Pin and stitch the front seam A–B.
3. Attach ½in (12mm) white lace to the lower leg hems and leave thread at each end to gather when fitted on to the doll.
4. Turn and stitch a ¼in (6mm) hem at the waist and again leave thread at each end to gather when fitted on to the doll.
5. Pin and stitch the back seam C–D.
6. With the *right sides together* form the pantaloon shape. Stitch the inside leg in one continuous operation.
7. Clip almost to the stitching line at the gusset before turning through to the right side and press.
8. Fit on to the doll and gather to fit the waist and above each section of porcelain leg.
9. Secure all threads and use to slip-stitch together the raw lace edges.

Petticoat

This is a pattern which will fit the four senior members of the staff.

1. Cut out the pattern or a strip of white cotton fabric 10in × 3in (25cm × 7.5cm) long.
2. Pin and stitch ¾in (20mm) wide white lace along one long edge to form the hemline. Press.
3. Using a large stitch, sew two rows across the waistline and leave threads at each end to gather when fitted on to the doll.

4. Pin and stitch the centre back seam, including the raw lace edges, leaving an opening 1¼in (30mm) at the waist.
5. Fit on to the doll and gather tightly into the waist. Secure all threads and slip-stitch the opening closed to complete.

Bodice

1. Cut out the bodice pattern pieces on double fabric – two front bodice, four back bodice – and transfer all the markings on to the fabric.
2. Cut out two sleeves and two cuffs and transfer any markings on to the fabric.
3. This is a basic pattern and so follow the instructions as given in Chapter 7. Before beginning construction decorate one front bodice with white lace so that all raw edges will be stitched into the shoulder seams.
4. Stitch across the top of the sleeves and across the lower edges of the sleeves and leave thread to gather at each end.
5. With the *right sides together* stitch the two side seams on each cuff. Turn through to the right side and press. It is helpful to stitch across the raw edges.
6. With the *right sides together* gather the lower edge of each sleeve on to a cuff. Pin and stitch.
7. Matching the centre top of the sleeves to the shoulder seams, ease the fullness between A and B. Pin and stitch.
8. With the *right sides together* form the bodice shape and stitch the side and sleeve seams in one continuous operation. Double stitch at the right angle underarm for strength and clip almost to point AB.
9. Turn the bodice through to the right side and press the side seams only.
10. Stitch a row of tiny beads (buttons) down the right back bodice and along each cuff.
11. Fit on to the doll and slip-stitch the centre back seam closed. Wrap each cuff as tightly as possible along the lower arm and slip-stitch into place.

Dress Skirt

1. Cut out the pattern or a strip of fabric 10in × 4in (25cm × 10cm) long.
2. Turn a ¼in (6mm) hem along one 10in (25cm) edge of the skirt to form the hemline.
3. Stitch two ⅛in (3mm) pin tucks close to the hemline.
4. Using a large stitch, sew two rows across the waistline and leave threads to gather.
5. Cut the waistband 3in × 1in (75mm × 25mm). Fold in half lengthways and with the *right sides together* stitch the side seams. Turn through to the right side and press.
6. Match the centre front skirt to centre waistband and gather evenly from each end. Pin and stitch. Press seam towards the hemline.
7. With *right sides together* pin and stitch the centre back seam, matching each pin tuck and leave an opening 1¼in (30mm) at the waist.

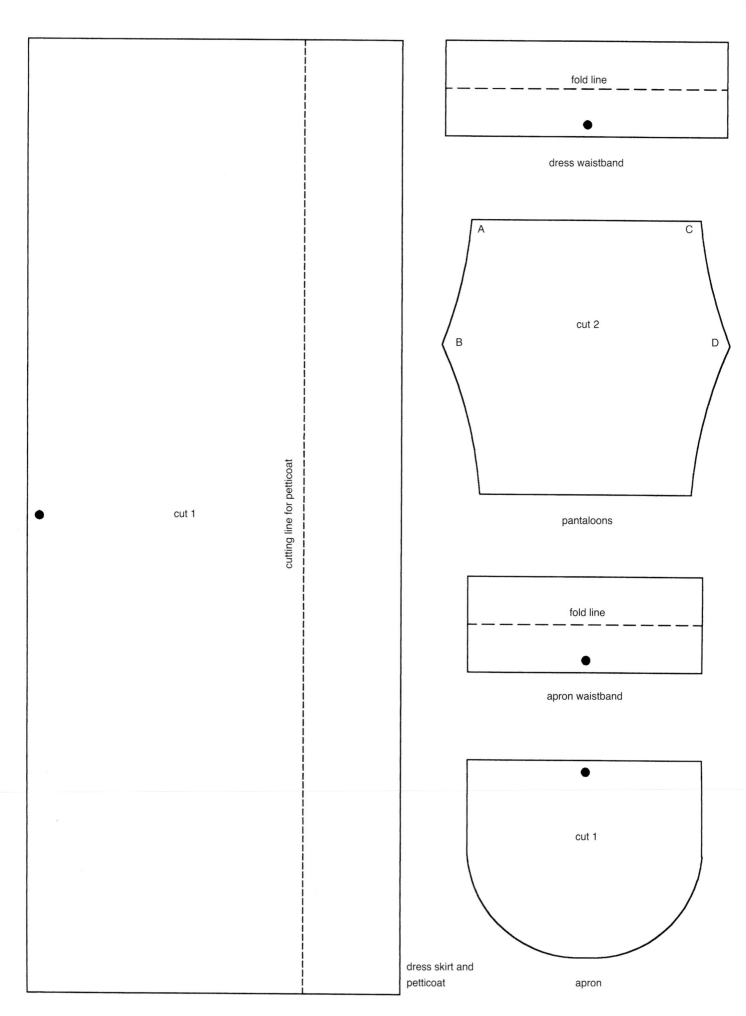

dress waistband

A   C

cut 2

B   D

pantaloons

cut 1

cutting line for petticoat

fold line

apron waistband

cut 1

apron

dress skirt and
petticoat

The housekeeper.

84

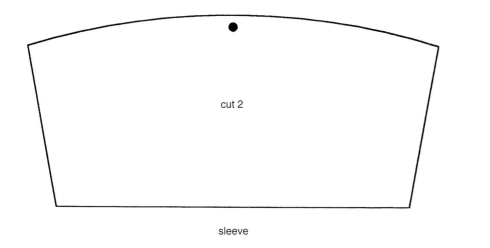

cut 2

sleeve

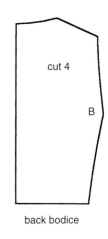

cut 4

B

back bodice

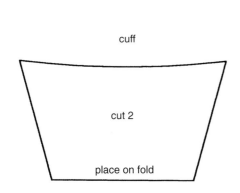

cuff

cut 2

place on fold

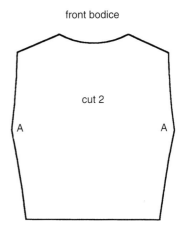

front bodice

cut 2

A   A

The housekeeper.

8. Fit on to the doll and stitch the waistband to secure into place. To complete, slip-stitch the opening closed.

Apron

1. Cut out the pattern on single fabric.
2. Slightly gather ¾in (20mm) wide white lace and attach round the curved edge of the apron.
3. Press the apron on the reverse side, ensuring that the seam lies inwards. Tack the seam into position.

4. Top stitch on the right side of the apron close to the fabric edge.
5. Using a large stitch, sew two rows across the top of the apron ready to gather.
6. Cut the waistband 2½in × 1in (65mm. × 25mm). Fold in half lengthways and at each end, insert from the inside a 6in (15cm) length of ¼in (6mm) white tape to make the ties.
7. Stitch across the side seams, securing the tapes. Turn through to the right side and press.
8. Gather the apron on to the waistband, pin and stitch.

Miss Stewart, the Governess

Wardrobe

- pantaloons
- petticoat
- fine, blue striped bodice/skirt
- full-length blue cape
- matching blue hat

Materials Required

- white cotton fabric
- fine, blue striped cotton fabric
- fine quality blue felt
- braid or ribbon for the hat trimming
- decorative braid or lace for the dress trimming
- fabric glue (since it is invisible when dry)

Pantaloons and Petticoat

Use the basic patterns and follow the instructions as given for the housekeeper.

Bodice

The instructions to make this garment are as given for the housekeeper. The only difference will be the decorative detail on the front of the bodice.

85

Miss Stewart, the governess.

Dress Skirt

1. Cut out the pattern or a strip of fabric 10in × 4¼in (25cm × 11cm) in length.
2. Turn a ¼in (6mm) hem along one 10in (25cm) edge of the skirt to form the hemline.
3. Stitch two ⅛in (3mm) pin tucks close to the hemline and 1in (25mm) apart.
4. Insert ¾in (20mm) decorative braid or lace under the second tuck and stitch into place.
5. Using a large stitch, sew two rows across the waistline and leave threads to gather.
6. Cut the waistband 3in × 1in (75mm × 25mm). Fold in half lengthways and with the *right sides together* stitch the side seams. Turn through to the right side and press.
7. Match the centre front skirt to the centre waistband and gather evenly from each end. Pin and stitch. Press seam towards the hemline.
8. With *right sides together* pin and stitch the centre back seam leaving an opening 1¼in (30mm) at the waist.
9. Fit on to the doll and stitch the waistband to secure into place. To complete, slip-stitch the opening closed.

Cape

1. Cut out the pattern on blue, middle-weight felt, remembering to place the centre back on a fold.
2. Mark the shoulder darts and the position of the hand slits with tailor tacking.
3. Tack and stitch the shoulder darts, cut down the centre of the darts and press flat. Trim any extra fabric from the darts around the neckline.
4. Turn ¼in (6mm) turnings on all edges. Tack and press on the inside of the garment.
5. Top stitch in one continuous line from the base of one front edge, around the neckline, down the opposite front edge and across the hemline.
6. Cut the hand slits (I found my stitch unpick to be ideal for this job; I also use it for buttonholes).
7. Cut two cuffs ¾in × 1½in (20mm × 35mm). Fold each lengthways and place a cuff with the fold to the front of the cape over each hand slit and tack into position. Top stitch round the three raw edges to secure into position.
8. Remove all tacking stitches and, if necessary, press lightly on the inside of the garment.

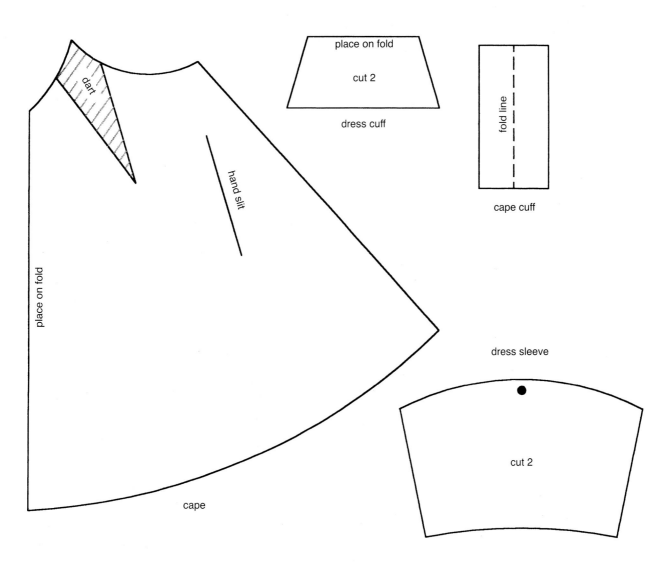

The governess.

87

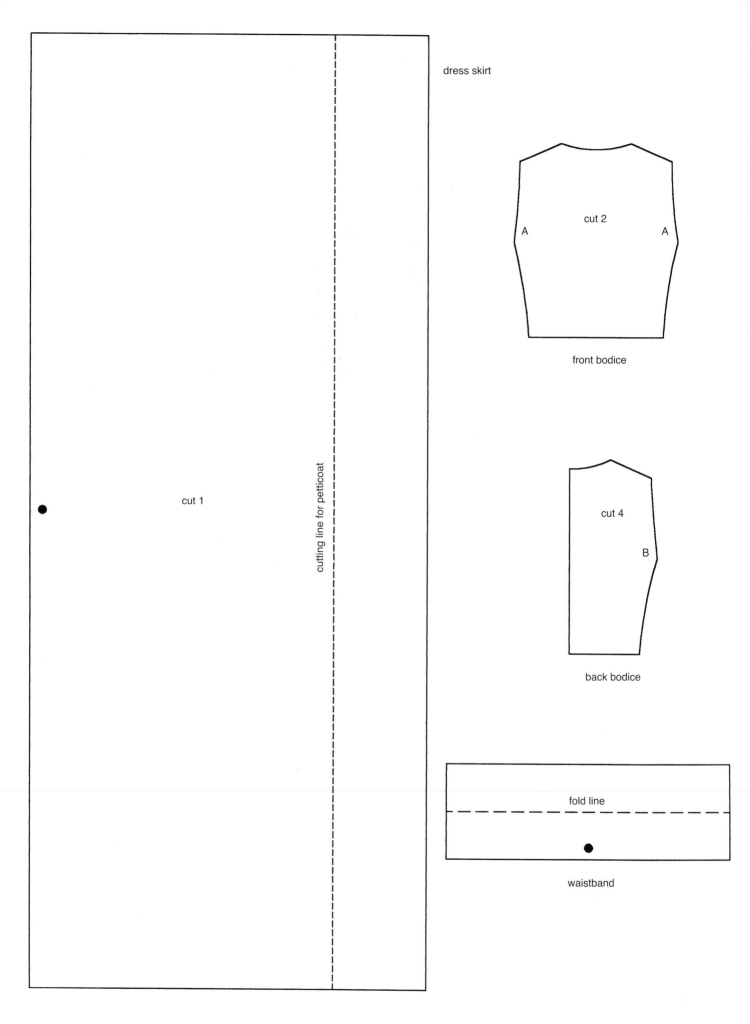

dress skirt

cut 1

cutting line for petticoat

cut 2

front bodice

A   A

cut 4

B

back bodice

fold line

waistband

The governess.

88

Miss Stewart with the children.

If fabric other than felt is to be used for the cape then it would be simplified if the whole garment were lined. First construct the outer cape, but do not cut the hand slits at this stage. Then construct a second cape in matching lining fabric. With the *right sides together* pin both front seams and around the neckline and almost along the hemline, but leave a sufficient gap at the cen-

tre back to turn the garment through to the right side. Tack and stitch in one continuous line. Turn through to the right side and press so that the lining is not visible around the edges. Slip-stitch across the gap at the centre back hemline. To complete, top stitch round the edge of the cape. Finally, cut the hand slits through both fabrics and immediately glue the lining into position (using the fabric glue). Complete the cuffs as above. If preferred, the hand slits may be omitted.

Cap

1. Cut a strip of matching felt 3½in × ½in (9cm × 12mm). The length required will vary according to the doll's head size and the hairstyle.
2. Fit the strip round the head in the position you wish the cap to be worn. (I opted for it to fit on top of the head, but pulled well down over the blonde fringe.)
3. A couple of dots of fabric glue, applied with a cocktail stick, will fix the circular shape of the hat; leave to dry.
4. Cut off any superfluous fabric and, using tiny stitches, over-sew each short cut edge to give a flat seam.
5. Find a button or coin that will sit on top of the circle of felt. Cut out a felt circle, apply glue sparingly below the edge only and press into position to form the crown.
6. Decorate the side of the cap with fancy black braid or ruched ribbon, leaving ties to fasten under the chin if desired.

Mrs Kitching, the Cook and Mrs Washington, Mistress of the Linen

Wardrobe

- pantaloons
- petticoat
- bodice/skirt
- white apron with pocket
- cook's cap and cuffs

Materials Required

- fine white cotton for underwear
- cotton fabric for dress: green, pink, blue or grey
- strong white cotton for the apron, cap and cuffs

Pantaloons and Petticoat

Use the patterns and follow the instructions as given for the housekeeper.

Bodice

1. Cut out the bodice pattern pieces on double fabric – two front bodice, four back bodice – and transfer all the markings on to the fabric.

2. Cut out two sleeves and transfer any markings on to the fabric.
3. For the *Mistress of Linen* cut out two cuffs.
4. This is a basic cotton bodice so follow the instructions as given in Chapter 7. The front bodice is enhanced with decorative stitching before beginning construction.
5. Stitch a row of gathering across the top of the sleeves ready to gather on to the bodice.
6. For the *Cook* turn a ⅛in (3mm) hem at the cuff edge of each sleeve. Pin, stitch and press.
7. For the *Mistress of Linen* stitch the two side seams on each cuff, turn through to the right side and press.
8. With the *right sides together*, evenly gather each sleeve on to a cuff. Pin and stitch.
9. Matching the centre top of the sleeves to the shoulder seams, ease fullness between A and B. Pin and stitch.
10. With the *right sides together* shape the bodice and stitch the side and sleeve seams in one continuous operation. Double stitch underarm for strength and clip almost to the stitching line. Turn through to the right side and press.
11. Fit on to the doll and slip-stitch the back seam. Complete with beads (buttons) down the centre back.

Mrs Kitching, the cook.

Mrs Washington, mistress of linen.

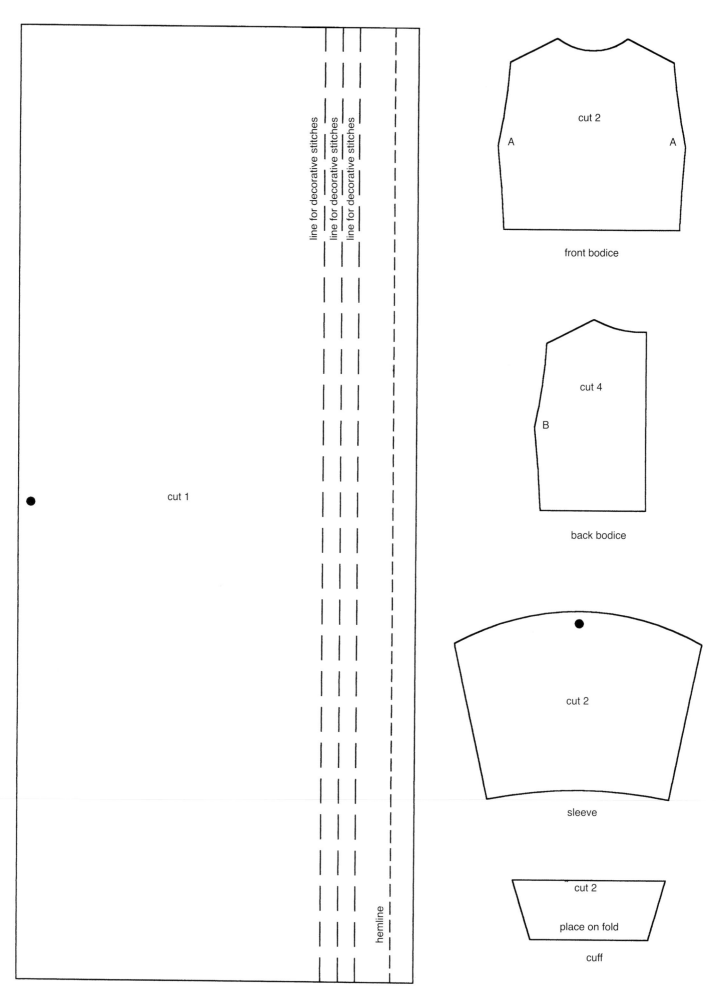

line for decorative stitches

line for decorative stitches

line for decorative stitches

hemline

cut 1

dress skirt

cut 2

A   A

front bodice

cut 4

B

back bodice

cut 2

sleeve

cut 2

place on fold

cuff

The cook.

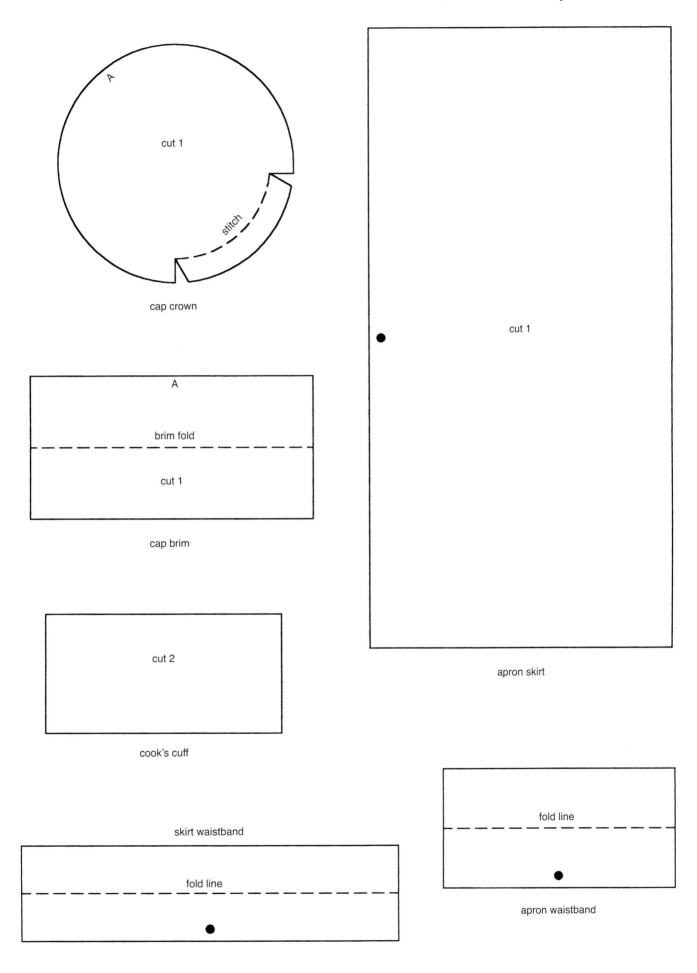

cap crown

cut 1

A

brim fold

cut 1

cap brim

cut 2

cook's cuff

cut 1

apron skirt

skirt waistband

fold line

fold line

apron waistband

The cook.

Dress Skirt

1. Cut out the pattern or a strip of fabric 10in × 4in (25cm × 10cm) in length.
2. Turn a ¼in (6mm) hem along one 10in (25cm) edge of the skirt to form the hemline.
3. For the *Cook* decorate the hemline with three to five rows of straight stitching using the spacing between the needle to edge of sewing foot as a guide.
4. For the *Mistress of Linen* stitch a ⅛in (3mm) pin tuck ¾in (20mm) above the hemline.
5. Using a large stitch, sew two rows across the waistline and leave threads to gather.
6. Cut the waistband 4in × 1¼in (10cm × 30mm). Fold in half lengthways and with the *right sides together* stitch the side seams. Turn through to the right side and press.
7. Match the centre front skirt to the centre waistband and gather evenly from each end, pin and stitch. Press seam towards hemline.
8. With *right sides together* pin and stitch the centre back seam, matching the decoration and leave an opening 1¼in (30mm) at the waist.
9. Fit on to the doll and stitch the waistband to secure in place. To complete, slip-stitch the opening closed.

Apron

1. Cut out the pattern or a strip of fabric 6½in × 3¼in (16cm × 8cm) in length.
2. Turn ¼in (6mm) hems along one long edge to form the hemline and both short sides.
3. Using a large stitch, sew two rows of gathering across the waistline.
4. Cut the waistband 2½in × 1¼in (65mm × 30mm). Fold in half lengthways and insert at both ends, from the inside, a 6in (15cm) length of ¼in (6mm) white tape to make the ties.
5. Stitch across the short sides, securing the tapes. Turn through to the right side and press.

6. Match centre apron to centre apron waistband, gather evenly from each end, pin and stitch.

Cook's Cuffs

1. Cut out the two cuffs 2½in × 1¼in (60mm × 30mm).
2. Turn a ¼in (6mm) hem on one long edge and leave thread to gather.
3. Stitch two rows across the opposite raw edge and leave thread to gather.
4. With the *right sides together* form a tube shape and pin and stitch the two side seams.
5. With the cuff still *wrong side outside* slip the raw edge over the hand and gather tightly round the wrist.
6. Pull the cuff up over the hand and lower sleeve and gather tightly; secure.

Cap

1. Cut out the crown piece and the brim. Mark points A with coloured thread.
2. One-quarter of the crown between the notches gathers into the back of the neck.
3. Stitch a line ¼in (6mm) from the raw edge between the two notches and leave thread to gather. Secure the thread at one end.
4. Stitch round the remaining circumference ¼in (6mm) from the raw edge and again leave thread to gather from either end.
5. Fold the brim in half lengthways and stitch the two side seams. Turn through to right side and press.
6. Match point A to point A and pin. Gather the crown evenly on to the brim from the two notches. Pin and stitch.
7. Snip the quarter curve a couple of times and fit the cap on to the doll. Gather the curve into the back of the neck, at the same time tucking the raw edge inside the stitching line.

The Household Maids

The set of patterns, comprising a bodice, a dress skirt, a petticoat, pantaloons, cuffs and a waistband, will fit all the young female members of the household staff – nursery maid, parlourmaid, housemaid and kitchen maid. Further sets of patterns and instructions give details for the individual caps and aprons.

Materials Required

Cotton fabrics in a selection of plain colours, small floral or checks and fine stripes. Traditionally black was always used for the parlourmaids.

Pantaloons

1. Cut out the pattern on double fabric and transfer all markings.
2. Pin and stitch the front seam A–B.
3. Attach narrow lace ½in (12mm) wide to the leg edges and leave enough thread at each end to gather when fitted on to the doll.
4. Turn and stitch a ¼in (6mm) hem at the waistline and leave thread at each end to gather.
5. Pin and stitch the back seam C–D.
6. With the *right sides together* form the pantaloon shape; stitch the inside leg in one continuous operation.
7. Clip almost to the stitching line at the gusset before turning through to the right side and press.
8. Fit on to the doll and gather tightly into the waist and above each section of porcelain leg. Secure all threads and use to slip-stitch the lace edges.

The household maids.

Petticoat

1. Cut out the pattern.
2. Attach narrow lace ½in (12mm) wide to one long edge to form the hemline. Press.
3. Leave to one side until required at a later step.

Bodice

1. Cut out the bodice pattern pieces on double fabric – two front bodice, four back bodice – and transfer all the markings on to the fabric.
2. Cut out two sleeves and transfer any markings on to the fabric.
3. For the *parlourmaid* and the *housemaid* cut out two cuffs. For the *nursery maid* and the *kitchen maid* turn a ⅛in (3mm) hem at the cuff edge of each sleeve.
4. This is a basic cotton bodice so follow the instructions as given in Chapter 7.

Dress Skirt

1. Cut out the pattern in the appropriate fabric and transfer all markings.
2. Turn a narrow hem along one long edge to form the hemline. Press.
3. Place the petticoat to the inside of the dress skirt and pin the waistline edges together.
4. Stitching through the double thickness, sew two gathering rows ⅛in (3mm) apart ready to gather on to the waistband.
5. With the *right sides together* fold the waistband in half lengthways and stitch the two side seams. Turn through to the right side and press.
6. Matching the centre front skirt to the centre of the waistband, gather the skirt and petticoat simultaneously on to the waistband, pin and stitch. Press seam upward.

7. With the *right sides together* pin and stitch the centre back seam of the dress skirt leaving an opening 1¼in (30mm) at the waist to fit.
8. Repeat the above with the petticoat and turn through to the right side. Press.
9. Fit on to the doll and stitch the waistband into position. To complete, slip-stitch the opening closed.

Aprons

Use the same pattern and method of construction for the apron bibs and waistbands, except for the *kitchen maid* (*see* later details). White cotton fabric is used for the majority of aprons except for that of the *kitchen maid* which is brown/grey.

1. Cut out the pattern for the bib ¾in (20mm) wide and 2½in (60mm) in length. Fold in half across the short side; the fold is the top of the bib.
2. Use a length of white bias binding 4¾in (12cm) long to enclose the sides of the bib and create a loop to pop over the doll's head. Tack and stitch the inside edge of the bias.
3. Cut out the waistband and fold ¼in (6mm) turnings on the two short sides before folding lengthways and pressing.
4. At each end of the waistband insert a length of narrow tape (a tie) and tack firmly into place.
5. Place centre bib (a) to centre waistband (a), with *all* raw edges together at (b) and tack firmly into position.
6. Top stitch the three folded sides of the waistband, securing into place the bib and ties in one operation.
7. With the *right sides together* pin centre apron (b) to centre waistband (b) and gather evenly from each side. Pin and stitch. Press.

PARLOURMAID

You will require a strip of broderie anglaise 6in (15cm) in length and 2¾in (7cm) in depth.

1. Turn a ¼in (6mm) hem along both short sides and press.
2. Using a large stitch, sew two rows of gathering across the raw edge ready to gather on to the waistband.

NURSERY MAID AND HOUSEMAID

1. Cut out the pattern on single fabric.
2. Turn a ¼in (6mm) hem along one long edge to form the hemline.
3. Stitch two ⅛in (3mm) pin tucks at ¾in (20mm) distance from the hemline.
4. Turn a ¼in (6mm) hem along both short sides.
5. Using a large stitch, sew two rows of gathering across the raw edge ready to gather on to the waistband.

KITCHEN MAID

1. Cut out the pattern on single fabric.

2. Turn a ¼in (6mm) hem across the top of the bib and round the apron skirt. Press and stitch.
3. Cut a bias strip 14in (35cm) long and turn in both long edges ¼in (6mm) to form a bias binding. Alternatively, purchase matching or contrast bias binding.
4. Fold the strip in half, allowing a 2in (50mm) loop to go over the head bind and tack the curved sides of the apron bib. Continue to each end of the bias to form the ties.
5. Machine stitch the whole length of the bias to complete the apron.
6. Add a pocket if you wish.

Caps

PARLOURMAID

She wears a mob cap.

1. Cut out the pattern in white cotton fabric.
2. Slightly gather a length of ½in (12mm) white lace and attach round the edge of the cap with the overlock or zigzag stitch (neatens and attaches in one operation).
3. If neither of the two above stitches is available, you will need to roll a narrow hem before attaching the lace.
4. Using a large machine stitch, circle the cap just inside the straight edge of the lace and leave thread to gather.
5. Fit the cap on to the doll and gather evenly to fit. Secure all threads on the inside of the cap.
6. Use narrow white ribbon to cover the gathering line and finish with a tiny bow to the rear.

NURSERY MAID

1. Cut out the cap brim 2½in × 1in (60mm × 25mm) in white cotton fabric.
2. Turn ¼in (6mm) hems on the two long edges and with the *right sides together* fold in half lengthways.
3. From the inside at both ends insert a 3in (75mm) length of narrow ribbon before stitching the two side seams. Turn through to the right side and press.
4. Slightly gather a length of ½in (12mm) white lace and insert the full length of the brim before stitching across to secure into place.

HOUSEMAID

1. Cut out the two pattern pieces and mark points A in coloured thread.
2. One quarter of the crown between the two notches gathers into the back of the neck.
3. Stitch a line between the notches ¼in (6mm) from the edge and leave thread to gather. Secure the thread at one end.
4. Stitch round remaining circumference ¼in (6mm) from the edge and leave threads to gather at either end.
5. With the *right sides together* fold the brim length-

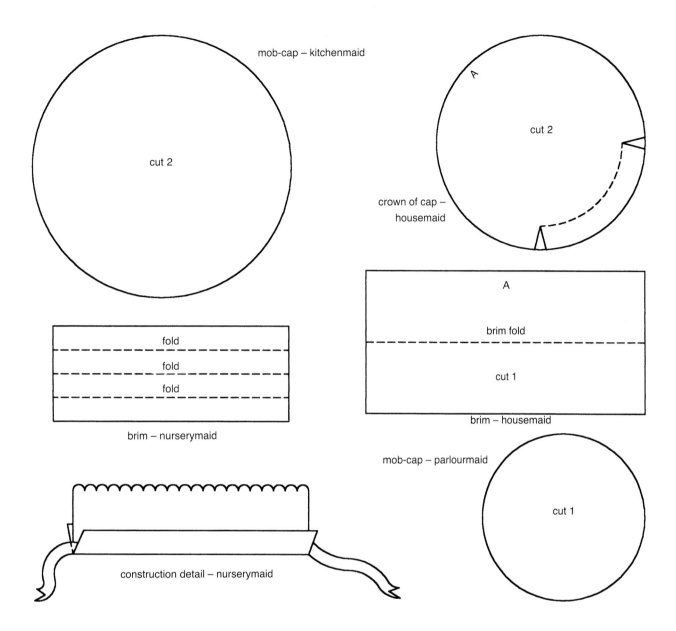

mob-cap – kitchenmaid

cut 2

A

cut 2

crown of cap –
housemaid

fold

fold

fold

brim – nurserymaid

A

brim fold

cut 1

brim – housemaid

mob-cap – parlourmaid

cut 1

construction detail – nurserymaid

ways and stitch the two side seams. Turn and press.

6. Match point A to point A and pin. Gather the crown evenly on to the brim from one notch to the second notch, pin and stitch.

7. Clip the quarter curve between the two notches and fit on to the doll. Gather the curve into the back of the neck; at the same time tuck the raw edge inside the stitching line.

KITCHEN MAID

She also wears a mob cap.

1. Cut out the pattern on double fabric.

2. With the *right sides together* stitch round the circumference leaving a small opening to turn through to the right side.

3. Clip round the edge of cap before turning through to the right side and slip-stitch the opening closed. Press.

4. Stitch a row of gathering ¼in (6mm) from the edge of cap and leave threads to gather.

5. Place on to the doll's head and gather evenly to fit. Secure all threads on the inside of cap.

6. Use narrow ribbon to cover the gathering line and finish with a tiny bow at the rear.

ABOVE: Maids' caps.
BELOW: Daisy, the tweeny.

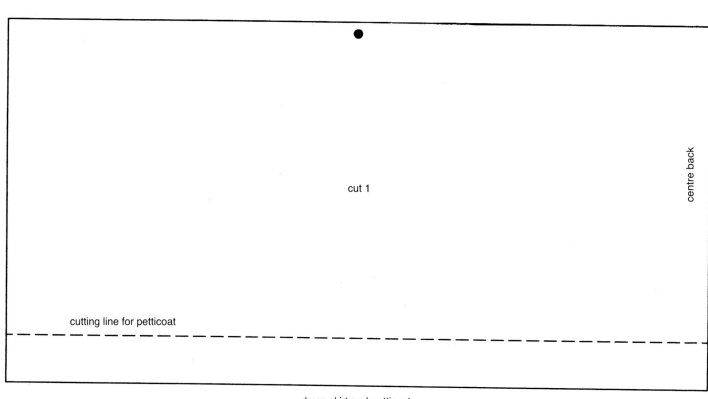

centre back

cut 1

cutting line for petticoat

dress skirt and petticoat

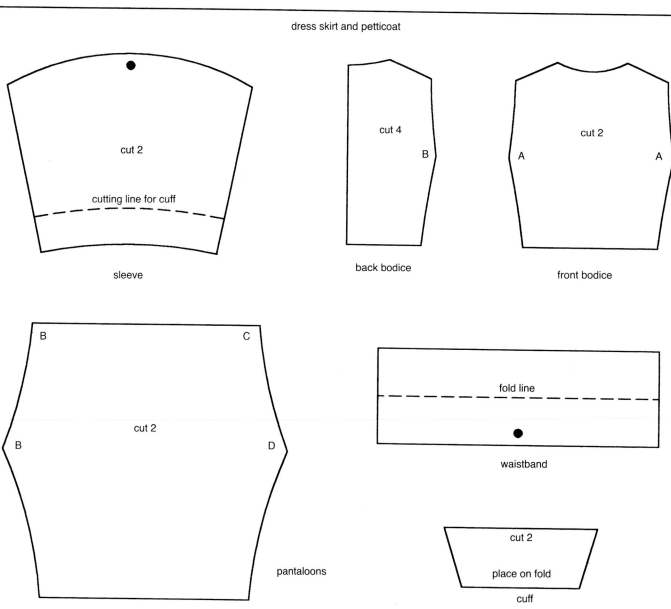

cut 2

cutting line for cuff

sleeve

cut 4

B

back bodice

cut 2

A   A

front bodice

B   C

cut 2

B   D

pantaloons

fold line

waistband

cut 2

place on fold

cuff

Household maids.

98

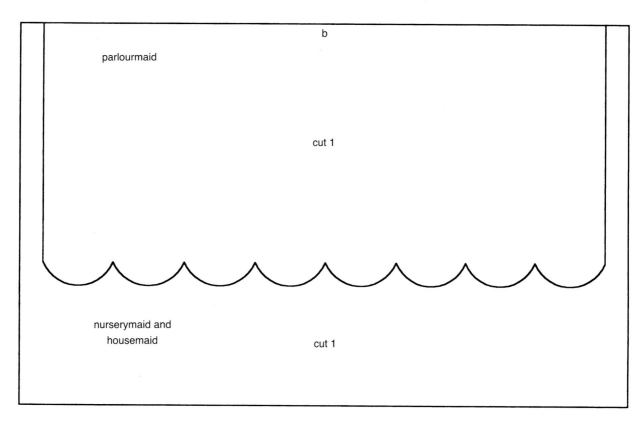

b

parlourmaid

cut 1

nurserymaid and
housemaid

cut 1

apron skirts

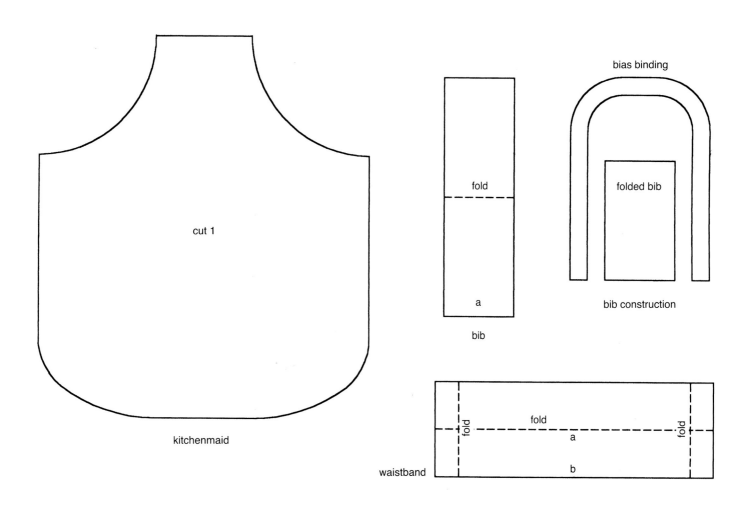

cut 1

kitchenmaid

bias binding

folded bib

bib construction

fold

a

bib

fold

fold

a

b

fold

waistband

Aprons.

Lady Pandora and Her Small Friends

There are two basic patterns in this section, but, by the use of different fabrics and a multiple of fabric designs, the dresses may be made to provide a variety. The decorated ribbon dress was inspired by an example seen at the Museum of Costume and Textiles in Nottingham, while the inspiration for the decorated tulle dress came from a pastel portrait of ten-year-old Lady Margaret Fife of Nunnington Hall in Yorkshire. In essence, the dresses are still of the two designs but quite different in appearance from the cotton prints. All the dresses can be created in cotton fabric, which I find the easiest medium, but, for that special-occasion look, then silk and taffeta come into their own. I found that the only way to work successfully with the smallest pattern pieces, that is, for the yoke, was to cut them out on bonded fabric. For this purpose I used a lightweight iron-on Vilene. This is also a useful hint for the no-frills petticoat bodice without turnings.

The child dolls may vary in height from 3½in (9cm) to 4½in (11cm) and to accommodate this range adjust the length of the bodice/yoke by ¼in (6mm) along the lower edge and then adjust the length of the dress skirts.

Patterns common to the child dolls are for the pantaloons, the petticoat and the pinafore. These are printed as one section. Note that the sleeves of the yoked dresses and the lace trim round the armholes of the pinafore are stitched by hand. This takes more time and some patience but I prefer the resulting appearance of the garments. It is possible to fit the sleeves as with all the previous patterns, that is, while the garment is placed flat on the working surface, but

you will have to accept side seams on the dress skirt and narrow shoulder seams on the pinafore. An additional pattern is included for this modification and the sequence of construction for the dress will be slightly different from the preferred model.

Pantaloons

These are a smaller version of those made for the adults, but I shall repeat the instructions here.

1. Cut out the pattern on double fabric and transfer all markings.
2. Pin and stitch the front seam A–B.
3. Attach narrow lace ¼in (6mm) wide to the leg hems and leave enough thread at each end to gather when fitted on to the doll.
4. Turn and stitch a ¼in (6mm) hem at the waistline and leave thread at each end to gather.
5. Pin and stitch the back seam C–D.
6. With the *right sides together* form the pantaloon shape, stitch the inside leg in one continuous operation.
7. Clip almost to the stitching line at the gusset before turning through to the right side and press.
8. Fit on to the doll and gather tightly into the waist and above each section of porcelain leg. Secure all threads and use to slip-stitch the lace edges.

Petticoat

This petticoat is made with a simple, no-frills bodice whose only function is to hold in place the petticoat skirt. When adjusted in length below the armhole it will fit neatly under both the yoked and the fitted waistline dresses. Version 1 is for yoked dresses and Version 2 for those dresses fitted on the waist.

Lady Pandora and her friends.

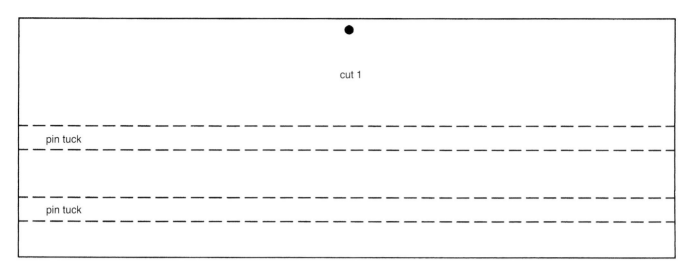

petticoat skirt – version 1

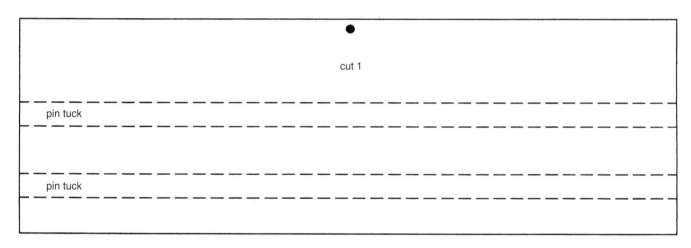

petticoat skirt – version 2

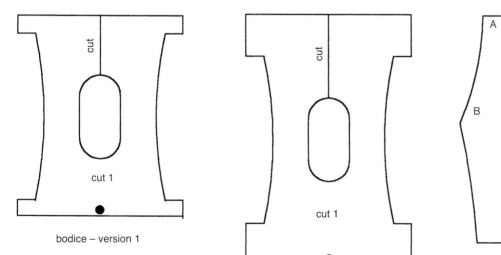

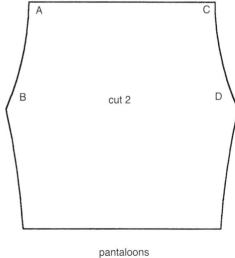

pantaloons

Girls' underclothes.

1. First draw the correct bodice for the required petticoat on the reverse side of the bonded fabric. Cut out the bodice and the matching skirt pattern and transfer all markings.
2. With the *right sides together* stitch the two short sides of the bodice, cut open the centre back seam and press. It is now ready to be attached to the skirt.
3. Attach narrow lace ½in (12mm) wide along one long edge of the skirt to form the hemline.
4. Stitch two narrow pin tucks above the lace edging; it is now ready to be attached to the bodice.

5. Using a large stitch, run two rows of gathering across the waistline. Matching centre front skirt to the centre front bodice, gather the skirt evenly from both ends on to the inside of the lower edge of the bodice to form a flat seam.
6. Pin and stitch with either an overlock or zigzag stitch. Press lightly.
7. With the *right sides together* pin the centre back seam of the skirt, matching the pin tucks and stitch.
8. Fit on to the doll and slip-stitch the centre back bodice seam closed.

Girls' pinafore.

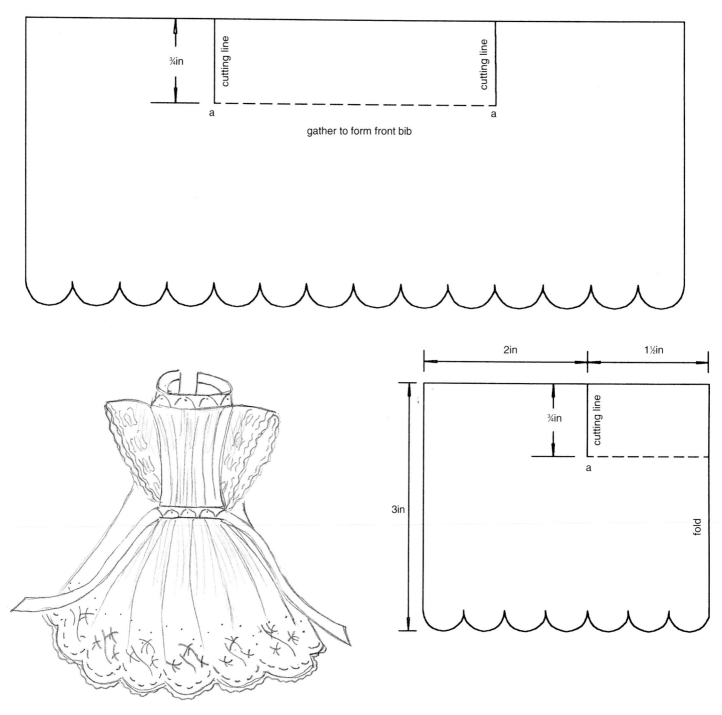

Pinafore

1. Cut a 7in × 3in (18cm × 75mm) length of broderie anglaise and turn a narrow hem on each short side.
2. Fold the strip in half (as in the diagram), and 1½in (35mm) from the centre line cut a ¾in (20mm) slit to form the armholes.
3. Using a large stitch, run two gathering lines across the top of each of the three individual sections and from a–a at centre front. Secure all threads at one end of each section.
4. Starting at the base of the armhole, attach slightly gathered ¾in (20mm) wide lace round each of the armholes, forming a tight loop at the shoulder (top) to complete the circle. Preferably this part of the garment should be hand-stitched. Run two rows of small stitches round the armhole before tidying the edges with blanket-stitch. Be sure to place the needle below the two rows of stitching in order to prevent the edge fraying. Apply Fray Stop.
5. Gather the rows of stitching across the centre section to form a bib 1¼in (30mm) in width.
6. Cut a 3in (75mm) length of bias binding. Gather the other two sections and with the bib fit into the folded bias and at the same time catch in the inner lace trim at the shoulder points and stitch.
7. An 11in (28cm) length of narrow ribbon will form the ties. Attach the centre of the ribbon to the centre front waist and stitch into position between a and a.
8. To complete, machine embroidery looks effective round the bias at the neckline and on the ribbon between a and a.

Lady Pandora Louise Vergette

This doll is 4½in (11.5cm) tall, clothed in a pretty Victorian party dress. Any little girl would feel like a princess when wearing it.

Wardrobe

- pantaloons
- petticoat, version 2
- dress

Materials Required

- fine white muslin/lawn cotton
- ⅜in (10mm) wide ivory-coloured lace
- ⅜in (10mm) wide ribbon.
- 1in (25mm) decorative ribbon for the bodice and hemline decoration
- brightly-coloured, contrasting ⅜in (10mm) ribbon for the sash

Pantaloons and Petticoat

Use the patterns common to the child dolls.

Dress

Two alternative sleeve patterns are included with this dress, but the length of the porcelain arms on the individual dolls will determine the use of the puff sleeve.

Bodice

1. Cut a 3½in × 1in (9cm × 25mm) length of the decorative ribbon, mark the position of the armhole slits where shown on the pattern and the centre front.
2. Turn and stitch a narrow hem on both short sides and leave until a later stage.

Dress Skirt

1. Cut out the skirt pattern and turn and stitch a narrow hem along one long edge to form the hemline. Press.
2. Decorate this piece of fabric with horizontal rows of ribbon, lace and pin tucks. Press the inside of the skirt each time a row of decoration is complete to avoid any ruching of the fabric.
3. When ready to gather on to the bodice, the length of the skirt needs to be 2½in (65mm).
4. Using a large stitch, run two rows of gathering across the waistline.
5. Match the centre front skirt to the centre front bodice and gather evenly from both ends on to the inside of the bodice to form a flat seam when stitched.
6. Cut the armhole slits marked on the bodice and pin the dress on to the doll. Use ⅜in (10mm) ribbon to form the shoulder straps such that the outer edge of the ribbon completes the armhole.
7. Cut out the sleeves and mark the centre top. Attach narrow lace to the cuff edges.
8. With the *right sides together* pin and stitch the sleeve seams. Turn and press.
9. Matching the top of the sleeve to the centre of the shoulder strap, ease the fullness to fit the armhole and stitch by hand into position.
10. With the *right sides together* pin and stitch the centre back seam of the skirt, matching all the rows of decorative detail. Leave an opening 1¼in (30mm) at the waist to fit on to the doll.
11. Fit the dress on to the doll and slip-stitch the centre back seam closed.
12. Run a row of small stitches round each cuff and gather tightly to form a lace ruffle.
13. It may be necessary to gather the inside of the shoulder straps to give a tight fit on to the neckline.
14. Complete with the addition of a contrasting coloured ribbon sash.

Lady Pandora Louise Vergette.

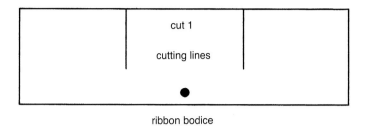

cut 1

cutting lines

ribbon bodice

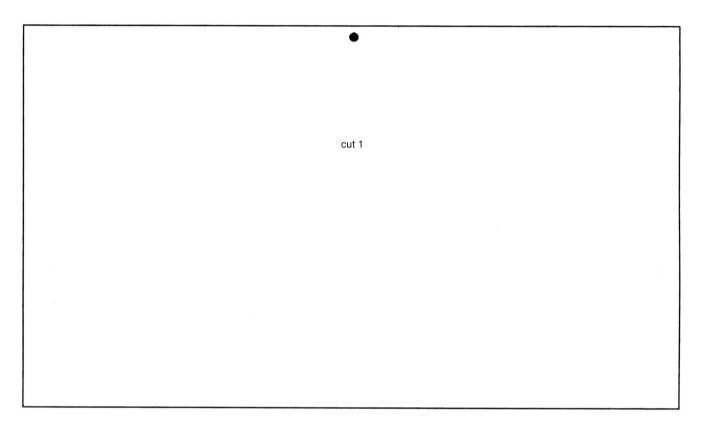

cut 1

dress skirt

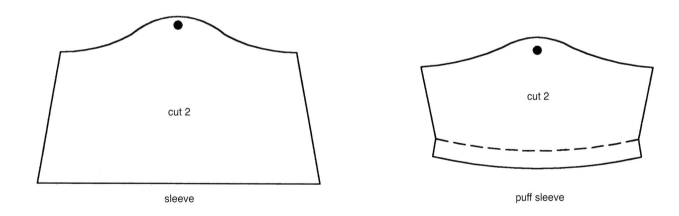

cut 2

sleeve

cut 2

puff sleeve

Pandora.

Lady Camilla Rose Fitzroy.

Lady Camilla Rose Fitzroy

This doll is also 4½in (11.5cm) tall. She wears a yoked dress, tailored in appliquéd tulle on silk, which presents a beautiful garment for a special occasion.

Wardrobe

• pantaloons
• petticoat, version 1
• dress

Materials Required

• fine ivory-coloured tulle as used for bridal veil
• fine ivory-coloured silk or tafetta for lining
• selection of ½in (12mm) wide laces
• narrow cream or contrasting ribbon

Pantaloons and Petticoat

Use the patterns common to the child dolls.

Dress

This is a fully-lined dress and care will need to be taken when cutting out the pattern as these fabrics tend to slip. Some initial preparation of the fabrics will assist in the making of the garment.

Prepare a 4in (10cm) square of fabric for use on the yoke in the following way. Pin a square of the fine tulle over the same of ivory silk. Appliqué the squares together either with a straight stitch or available fancy stitch. The rows of stitching may be vertical, horizontal or oblique and approximately ⅛in (3mm) apart.

Prepare an 8in × 4in (20cm × 10cm) rectangle of tulle with horizontal rows of ribbon and lace, either in the same colour or with a pastel contrast. Begin by turning a ½in (12mm) hem along one long edge to form the hemline, tack into place and stitch the first row of lace to hold permanently in position. It is easier on this style of dress to add the yoke lace and ribbon trim as a final stage.

1. Cut out the yoke pattern once in the appliqué fabric and a second time in plain fabric for the lining.

2. Construct the yoke as the instructions given for the basic bodice in Chapter 7 in order to give a professional finish to the neckline and back opening. Press with a warm iron.

3. Cut out the skirt pattern once in the horizontally-decorated tulle and a second time in plain fabric for the lining. Mark the armhole slits. Note that there is an allowance on the pattern to turn a narrow hem on the lining; the tulle is already hemmed. Turn the hem on the lining and place the tulle over, securing in place with several rows of tacking. Check that the skirt is 7in × 2¾in (18cm × 7cm) and that the armhole slits match before cutting. The skirt is now ready to be attached to the yoke.

4. Using a large stitch, run two rows of gathering across the top of each section of the skirt.

5. With the *right sides together* pin the centre front skirt to the centre front yoke and gather this section on to front yoke. Pin and stitch.

6. Gather the two back sections of the skirt on to the back yoke in the same way. Press the seams towards the neckline.

7. Cut out the sleeve pattern on double plain fabric and mark the centre top sleeve.

8. Attach narrow lace to the cuff edges and run a gathering line across the top of the sleeves.

9. With the *right sides together* pin and stitch the sleeve seams, including the lace edgings. Turn and press.

10. With the *right sides together*, but working from the inside of the dress, match the top of the sleeves to the shoulder seams and ease the fullness to fit the armhole. Pin and stitch by hand into place. Use blanket stitch to neaten the raw edges, making sure to insert the needle below the fixing stitches in order to prevent fraying. Apply Fray Stop.

11. Add the lace and ribbon decoration round the yoke and stitch into place, through all thicknesses, either by hand or by machine. It is easy to machine stitch as the centre back seam of the dress will still be open, allowing the dress to be placed flat under the needle foot.

12. With the *right sides together* pin and stitch the centre back seam, matching all decorative detail and leaving an opening of 1¼in (30mm) to fit on to doll.

13. Fit the dress on to the doll and slip-stitch the centre back seam closed.

14. Run tiny stitches round the top of lace on each cuff and gather to form ruffles. Secure all threads.

Camilla.

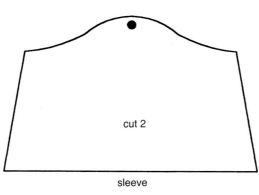

sleeve

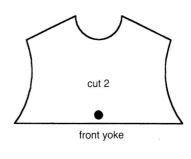

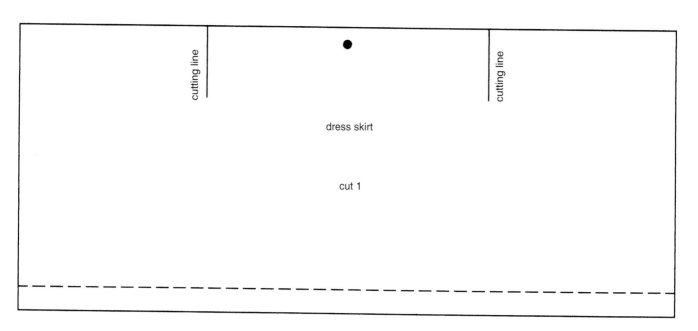

cutting line

cutting line

dress skirt

cut 1

Camilla.

Miss Verity Patience Carlisle

The doll is again 4½in (11.5cm) tall. She wears a yoked dress tailored in single fabric but of essentially the same construction as for that of Lady Camilla Rose.

Wardrobe

- pantaloons
- petticoat, version 1
- dress

Materials Required

- royal blue silk or taffeta fabric, preferably with a tiny self pattern
- white cotton for contrasting yoke, with tiny self pattern
- white lawn for underclothes
- ½in (12mm) wide white lace
- narrow scarlet ribbon for the yoke trim

Pantaloons and Petticoat

Use the patterns common to the child dolls.

Dress

Two alternative sleeve patterns are included with this dress, but the length of the porcelain arms on the individual dolls will determine the use of the puff sleeve.

Prepare a 4in (10cm) square of the contrasting yoke fabric by bonding on to lightweight iron-on Vilene or similar. It is easier on this style of dress to add the yoke lace and ribbon trim as a final stage.

1. Cut out the yoke pattern once in the contrasting bonded fabric and a second time in non-bonded fabric. Remember that it is often easier to draw round the small pattern pieces and then cut out rather than to try to cut out with the pattern pinned to the fabric.
2. Construct the yoke as the instructions given for the basic bodice in Chapter 7 in order to give a professional finish to the neckline and back opening. Press with a warm iron.
3. Cut out the skirt pattern and mark the slits for the armholes and the centre front.
4. Turn a narrow hem along one long edge to form the hemline, stitch and press.
5. Stitch one ⅛in (3mm) pin tuck ¾in (20mm) above the hemline and insert a length of ½in (12mm) lace under the pin tuck to complete the skirt trim.
6. Cut the slits for the armholes. The skirt is now ready to be attached to the yoke.
7. Follow stages 4 to 7 as given in the pattern for Lady Camilla.
8. Fold the cuff edge of the sleeve where shown on the pattern and stitch. This double edge will later form the plain ruffle at the wrist.
9. Using a large stitch, run a gathering line across the top of the sleeves.
10. With the *right sides together* pin and stitch the sleeve seams, including the turning for the ruffle.
11. Follow stages 10 to 13 as given in the pattern for Lady Camilla.
12. Run two rows of tiny stitches round the plain cuff at ¼in (6mm) spacing from the folded edge. Draw up tightly to form a ruched ruffle at the wrist.

These are the instructions for the alternative construction of the yoked dress allowing for the sleeves to be attached while the garment can be laid flat on the work surface.

1. Cut out the pieces for the alternative pattern and transfer all markings.
2. Construct the yoke as described earlier.
3. Using a large stitch, run two gathering lines across the top of each skirt section.
4. With the *right sides together* pin the centre front skirt to the centre front yoke and gather this section on to the front yoke. Pin and stitch.
5. With the *right sides together* pin and stitch the centre back seam to point C and press open.
6. With the *right sides together* attach the back skirt to the back yoke.
7. Open the garment and, by using the edge of the ironing board, press the yoke seams towards the neckline.
8. Fold the cuff edge of the sleeve where shown on the pattern and stitch. This double edge will later form the plain ruffle at the wrist.
9. Using a large stitch, run a gathering line across the top of the sleeves.
10. Matching the centre top of the sleeves to the shoulder seams, ease fabric between A and B. Pin and stitch.
11. With the *right sides together* shape the dress and pin and stitch the sleeve and side seams in one continuous operation.
12. Clip the side seam underarm almost to point AB before turning through to the right side and press.
13. Turn a narrow hem ¼in (6mm) round the hemline and stitch.
14. Alternatively, the skirt may be shortened and a flounce added to the hemline. Use double fabric for the flounce such that the fold forms the lower edge.
15. Add further decorative detail if required.

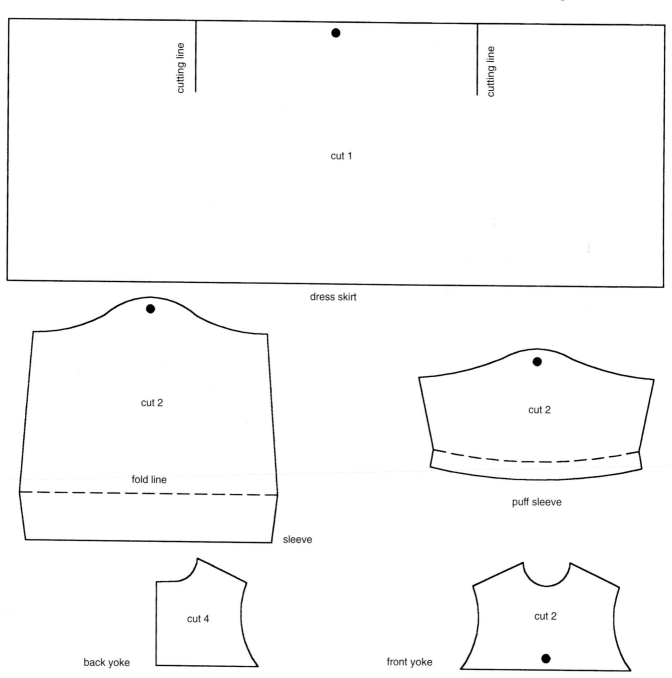

cutting line

cutting line

cut 1

dress skirt

cut 2

fold line

sleeve

cut 2

puff sleeve

cut 4

back yoke

cut 2

front yoke

Verity.

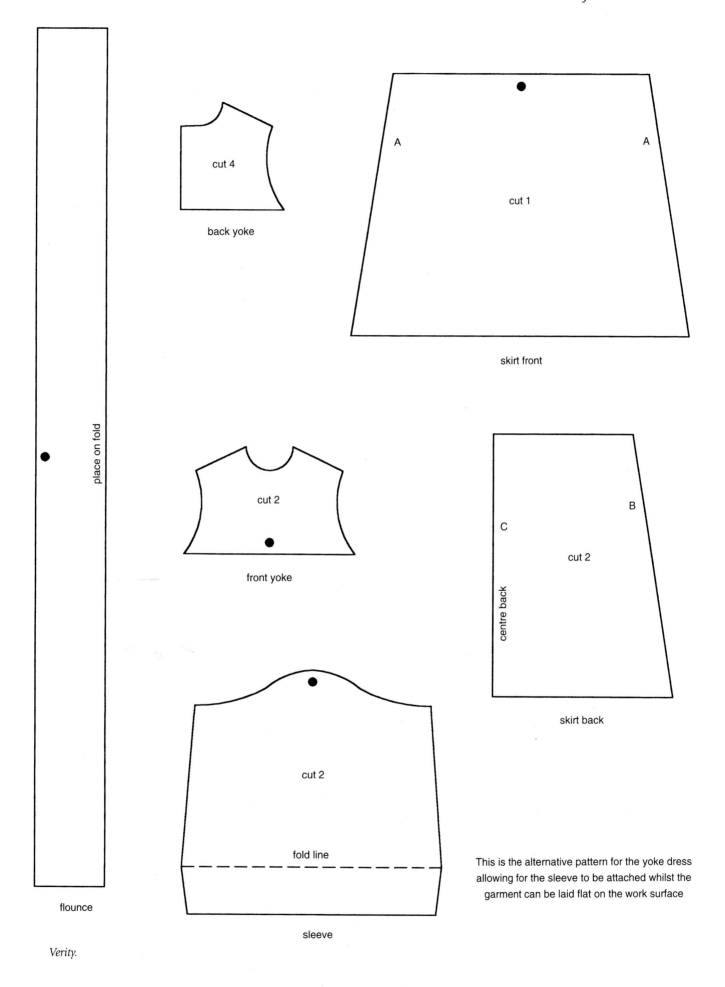

place on fold

cut 4

back yoke

A   A

cut 1

skirt front

cut 2

front yoke

B

C

cut 2

centre back

skirt back

cut 2

fold line

This is the alternative pattern for the yoke dress
allowing for the sleeve to be attached whilst the
garment can be laid flat on the work surface

flounce

Verity.

sleeve

The Hon. Venetia Rosemary Wallis and Miss Claire Nicholson-Walker

These dolls are also both 4½in (11.5cm) tall. Venetia wears a dress of lavender colour and Claire one of pink. This is a dress with a fitted waistline to wear beneath a decorative pinafore.

Wardrobe

- pantaloons
- petticoat, version 2
- dress
- broderie anglaise pinafore

Materials Required

- fine cotton fabric with a tiny floral pattern
- fine white cotton fabric for the underwear
- 3in (75mm) wide broderie anglaise with a small design
- selection of narrow lace to trim the underwear
- ⅛in (3mm) white satin ribbon
- white bias binding

Pantaloons and Petticoat

Use the patterns common to the child dolls.

Bodice

1. Cut out the pattern pieces on double fabric and transfer all markings.

2. This is a basic bodice so follow the instructions given in Chapter 7.
3. Attach ½in (12mm) lace to the cuff edges of the sleeves and leave thread at each end to gather at a later stage.
4. Using a large stitch, run a gathering line across the top of the sleeves. Matching the centre top of the sleeves to the shoulder seams, ease fullness between A and B. Pin and stitch.
5. With the *right sides together* form the bodice shape and stitch the side and sleeve seams in one continuous operation. Double stitch at the right angle underarm for strength and clip almost to point AB.
6. Turn through to the right side and press the side seams only.

Dress Skirt

1. Cut out the pattern and mark the centre front of the skirt at the waistline.
2. Turn a narrow hem ¼in (6mm) along one long edge to form the hemline.
3. Using a large stitch, run two gathering rows across the waistline ready to attach on to the bodice.
4. With the *right sides together* match the centre front of the skirt to the centre front of the bodice and pin.
5. Gather the skirt evenly from either end on to the bodice, pin and stitch.
6. With the *right sides together* pin and stitch the centre back seam of the dress to point C.
7. Fit the dress on to the doll and slip-stitch the centre back seam closed up to the neckline.
8. Gather the threads tightly at the wrists to form lace ruffles and secure all threads.

Pinafore

Use the patterns common to the child dolls.

Venetia Rosemary Wallis and Claire Nicholson-Walker.

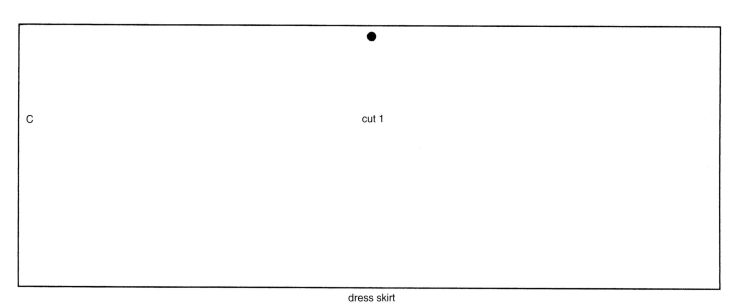

C   cut 1

dress skirt

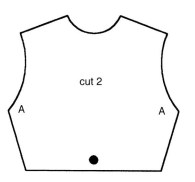

cut 2

A   A

front bodice

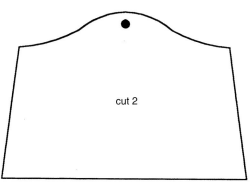

cut 2

sleeve

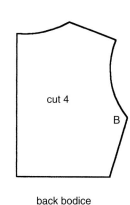

cut 4

B

back bodice

Venetia and Claire.

Nicholas William Vergette

This doll is 4in (10cm) tall and wears a sailor suit.

Wardrobe

- trousers
- sailor blouse
- sailor collar
- straw boater

Materials Required

- plain blue cotton and white cotton
- fine blue/white-striped cotton
- ⅛in (3mm) ribbon

Trousers

1. Cut out the pattern on double fabric and transfer all markings.

2. With the *right sides together* pin and stitch the front seam A–B. Open the seam and press.
3. Turn a ¼in (6mm) hem along the lower edge of each trouser leg. Tack, stitch and press. Alternatively, these hems may be bonded by using iron-on Vilene or similar.
4. Using a large stitch, run two rows of gathering across the waistline.
5. With the *right sides together* pin and stitch the back seam C–D. It is possible to slightly adjust this seam at a later stage.
6. With the *right sides together* form the trouser shape and stitch the inside leg in one continuous operation. Double stitch in the gusset area for strength.
7. Clip almost to the stitching line at the gusset before turning through to the right side and press.
8. Fit on to the doll; if necessary adjust the back seam before gathering to a snug fit and secure the threads.

Sailor Blouse

This is an over-blouse and the hemline is gathered into the body to give a blouson effect.

Nicholas William Vergette.

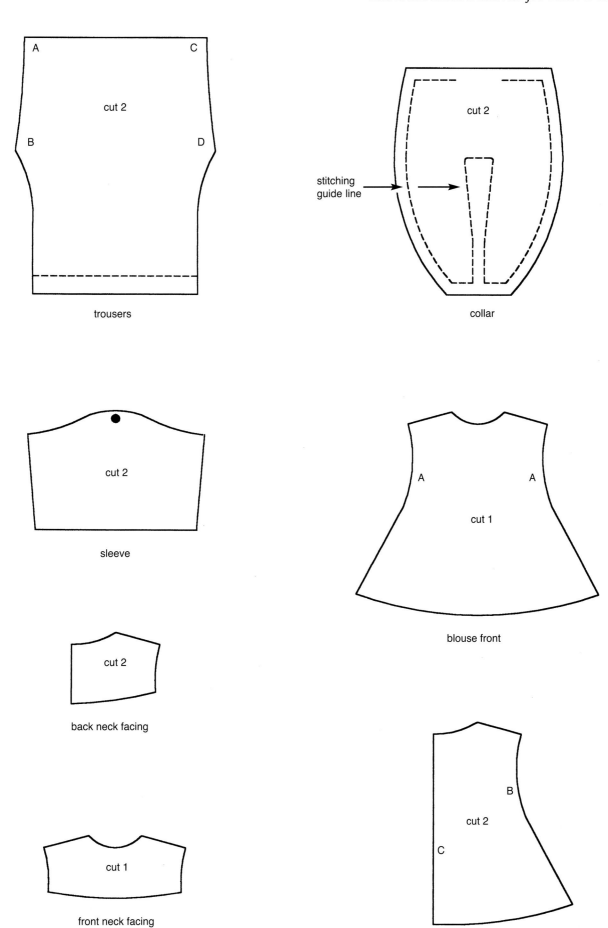

A C

cut 2

B D

trousers

cut 2

stitching
guide line

collar

cut 2

sleeve

A A

cut 1

blouse front

cut 2

back neck facing

cut 1

front neck facing

B

cut 2

C

blouse back

Sailor suit.

1. Cut out the pattern pieces and transfer all markings on to the fabric.
2. With the *right sides together* join the front blouse to the two back blouse at the shoulder seams. Open the seams and press.
3. With the *right sides together* join the front neck facing to the back neck facings at the shoulder seams. Open the seams and press.
4. With the *right sides together* stitch the neck facing to the blouse round the neckline. Clip almost to the stitching line before turning the facing to the inside and press.
5. Secure the neck facing to the armhole edges.
6. With the *right sides together* and matching the top of the sleeves to the shoulder seams, ease fabric between A and B. Pin and stitch.
7. With the *right sides together* form the blouse shape and stitch the sleeve and side seams in one continuous operation.
8. Clip the side seam underarm almost to point AB before turning through to the right side and press.
9. Using a large stitch, run a gathering line at ¼in (6mm) distance from the hemline and leave threads to gather.
10. With the *right sides together* stitch the lower back seam to point C. Open the seam and press.
11. Fit the blouse on to the doll and slipstitch the back seam closed.
12. Pull the gathers to form the blouson effect and at the same time tuck the raw edges of the hemline inside the blouse. Secure the threads.
13. Gather the raw cuff edges tightly round the wrists and cover with white cuffs. Use white ribbon or white bias tape

14. Stitch four or five bugle beads to represent buttons down the back seam.

Sailor Collar

1. Cut out the pattern on double fabric.
2. Beginning close to the centre back, stitch round the collar, following the stitch guideline but leave a sufficient gap to turn through to the right side. Note that now is the time to cut out the inner neckline. By leaving to this stage it prevents the movement of the fabric as you stitch.
3. Clip the curved edges of the collar and turn through to the right side. Press and slip-stitch the opening closed.
4. Decorate the outer edge of the collar with a line of straight stitching using navy cotton. Alternatively, use 2mm wide ribbon.
5. Fit the collar round the doll's neck and secure the two front points with a few stitches into the blouse front.
6. Complete with a tie of ⅛in (3mm) red ribbon placed under the collar and purchase a tiny straw boater.

Girl's Dress

The sailor fashion was equally popular with young girls. The sailor blouse above may be teamed with a pleated skirt in either navy or white fabric. For ease, use the kilt pattern as given below for the Osbourne twins and use white or navy ribbon.

The Hon. Digby Spencer

This doll is 4½in (11.5cm) tall and wears a Norfolk suit.

Wardrobe

- breeches
- jacket
- shirt collar

Materials Required

- fine white lawn
- small-checked fabric either cotton or worsted
- black/brown glove leather for belt
- tiny black beads and buckle

Breeches

1. Cut out the pattern on double fabric and transfer all markings.

2. Pin and stitch the front seam A–B and press. Turn a ¼in (6mm) hem at the waistline, stitch and press.
3. Pin and stitch the back seam C–D.
4. With the *right sides together* form the breeches shape and stitch the inside leg in one continuous operation.
5. Turn through to the right side and press the inside seam, but avoid creasing the outer leg.
6. Fit on to the doll and tightly gather each leg above the porcelain section. If possible, tuck the raw edges down into the leg.
7. From bonded fabric cut a ¼in (6mm) strip of fabric to use for the knee cuffs.
8. Glue the cuffs round the top of the porcelain legs, ensuring that they are in close contact with the breeches. Place the joins to rear of the legs.
9. Stitch a button on the outside of each cuff.

Jacket

1. Cut out the pattern pieces, the front and back only on bonded fabric and transfer all markings.
2. With the *right sides together* pin and stitch the jacket fronts to the back at the shoulder seams. Press the seams open.

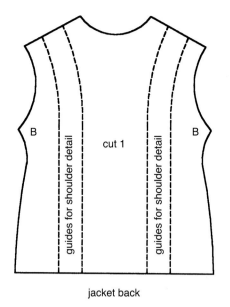

jacket back

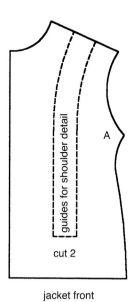

jacket front

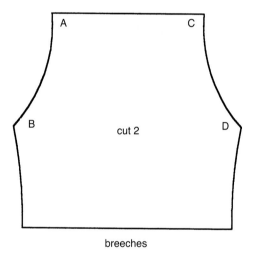

breeches

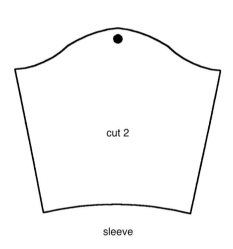

sleeve

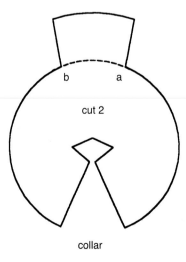

collar

Norfolk suit.

118

3. Cut two 4in × ¼in (100mm × 6mm) strips of bonded self-material and use them to create the over-the-shoulder detail.
4. Pin the strips into position where indicated on the pattern guides and stitch the full length along the inside edges, those closest to the centre of the jacket.
5. Turn ⅛in (3mm) hems at the cuff edges of the sleeves. Pin and stitch or bond into position.
6. Run a gathering row of stitching across the top of the sleeves.
7. Matching the top of the sleeves to the shoulder seams, ease the fullness between A and B, pin and stitch.
8. With the *right sides together* form the jacket shape and stitch the side and sleeve seams in one continuous operation.
9. Clip the side seam underarm almost to point AB before turning through to the right side and press.
10. Turn ⅛in (3mm) facing down the left front of the jacket and stitch.
11. Stitch six buttons, evenly spaced, on the *left* side of the jacket front.
12. Cut a strip of ¼in (6mm) leather to use for the belt.
13. Fit the jacket on to the doll and at the rear waistline cut two or three of the stitches in the shoulder detail to form the belt loops. Insert the belt and bring both ends to the front and repeat the operation to form the front loops. Fit a buckle to one end of the belt and adjust the length to fit.
14. Slip-stitch the front of the jacket from neckline to waistline.

Shirt Collar

1. Cut out the pattern on double fabric – the tab is to help when turning the collar through to the right side – and transfer all markings.
2. With the *right sides together* stitch all round the edge of the collar from a to b.
3. Clip the curved edges before turning the collar through to the right side.
4. Reduce the tab by half in length, and fold the raw edges inside to close the collar and complete the shape. Slip-stitch the opening closed.
5. Press flat before placing round the doll's neck, over the jacket, and secure under the chin.
6. Complete with a floppy black bow.

The Osbourne Twins

These are both 4½in (11.5cm) tall. The idea for the twins came from a photograph of Queen Victoria's younger sons in Highland dress for the wedding of their elder brother Edward, Prince of Wales to Alexandra of Denmark in 1863. This, as other similar occasions had done, created a popular fashion in children's wear throughout the Empire.

Wardrobe

- Highland kilt
- black coatee
- shirt sleeves
- lace jabot
- sporran
- shoulder drape
- tam-o'-shanter

Materials Required

- 1yd (1m) of 1½in (38mm) tartan ribbon
- ½yd (0.5m) of ½in (12mm) matching tartan ribbon
- black cotton fabric or felt
- ½in (12mm) white lace
- ½in (12mm) black cotton bias tape
- ¼in (6mm) scarlet ribbon
- tiny gold beads
- brown or black glove leather
- small fur pieces

Socks

The socks are represented by adding stocking tops to the prepainted boots on the porcelain legs of the doll.

1. Put a thin line of glue round the top of the boot.
2. Using ½in (12mm) black bias tape, begin at the back of the leg and wrap the bias twice round the top of the boot, inserting a tab of scarlet ribbon between the two layers on the outside of the leg.
3. Continue to bind to halfway up the leg and finish at the rear, fix in place with a spot of glue.

Plaid Shorts

Use the 1½in (38mm) tartan ribbon as the fabric. On this garment the waist and leg edges are formed neatly by the two selvedges of the ribbon.

1. Cut out the pattern on double ribbon.
2. Pin and stitch the front seam A–B.
3. Pin and stitch the back seam C–D.
4. With the *right sides together* shape the shorts and stitch the inside of the leg in one continuous operation.
5. Turn through to the right side and press.

Kilt

1. Use a 10in (25cm) length of the 1½in (38mm) ribbon and follow the diagram to form the ¼in (6mm) pleats.
2. Work on the flat surface of an ironing board so that you can fix each pleat, top and bottom, with a pin pushed into the soft top.

The Osbourne twins.

3. When all the pleats are in place, press with a hot iron over a double thickness of cotton, since both silk and taffeta are delicate fabrics.
4. When the fabric has cooled, place a strip of Sellotape or similar material across the centre of the pleats to hold in place.
5. Remove all the pins and stitch across the waist edge to hold the pleats in position.
6. Further secure each individual pleat by stitching for ½in (12mm) from the waist to the hip. Pull all threads through to the inside of the kilt and knot securely.
7. Measure 1in (25mm) for the underflap and stay-stitch a vertical line, either zigzag or overlock, before cutting off any superfluous ribbon.
8. Repeat the above for the front overlap but leave ⅛in (3mm) of the ribbon to create the fringe.
9. Fit on to the doll, over the tartan shorts, and oversew the underflap and the front overlap across the front waist.
10. To hold the kilt at the correct length, fix it to the body at the centre front and centre back with a few stitches.

Shirt Sleeve

1. Cut out the pattern on double fabric.
2. Attach ½in (12mm) white lace to the cuff edges.
3. With the *right sides together* pin and stitch the sleeve seam. Turn and press.
4. Fit the sleeves on to the doll and gather tightly at the wrists to form lace ruffles.
5. Pin the top of the sleeves to the finger bandage round the top of the arms and hand stitch to hold in place.

Coatee

1. Cut out the back and two front pattern pieces on bonded black cotton fabric or felt and transfer all markings.
2. Cut out the sleeves on non-bonded fabric and mark the centre top sleeve.
3. Turn a narrow hem at the cuff, pin and stitch or bond into place.
4. With the *right sides together* join the two front coats to the back at the shoulder seams. Pin and stitch. Open the seams and press flat.
5. Matching the centre top of the sleeves to the shoulder seams, ease the fullness between A and B. Pin and stitch.
6. With the *right sides together* form the coatee shape and stitch sleeve and side seams in one continuous operation.
7. Double stitch under the arm for strength and clip almost to point AB before turning through to the right side and press.

8. Stitch six or eight gold buttons to the *left* side of the coatee. Fit on to the doll and slip-stitch the front closed.

Jabot

Attaching lace to a short length of ⅛in (3mm) ribbon creates this item. Owing to its very small size, you may wish to start with a longer length of ribbon before cutting to the correct size, as shown in the diagram.

1. Starting at 1in (25mm) from the end of the ribbon, gather ½in (12mm) white lace on to the underside and work towards the end, crossing the front of the ribbon to leave a ¼in (6mm) tab behind the lace and continue up the other side to match.
2. Cut the ribbon to match the raw edges of the lace and turn a ⅛in (3mm) hem to neaten.
3. Take a piece of ribbon slightly longer than the dimension of the neck of the doll and attach the jabot to one end. Adjust to fit the neck and glue in place with the join concealed under the lace.

Sporran

1. Cut out the pouch pattern from soft glove leather.
2. Cut a length of leather strip ⅛in (3mm) wide to use as the waist belt, allowing the sporran to hang low at the front of the kilt.
3. With the *wrong sides together* glue the belt into place, as shown on the pattern.
4. Cover the pouch below the belt with fur and fix with glue.
5. Fold the pouch flap over the belt and secure into place. Fit on to the doll.

Shoulder Drape

1. Cut an 8in (20cm) length of ½in (12mm) tartan ribbon.
2. Fold in half, place the fold under the right arm and bring both ends of the ribbon to meet over the left shoulder and stitch.
3. Fold both ends of the ribbon down to the front and trim obliquely to the required length.
4. Create the shoulder brooch/pin by attaching five tiny pearl/bugle beads.

Girl's Dress

Teamed with a frilled or lace-trimmed white blouse, the Highland kilt would also be worn by young girls. Use the pattern as given for the child's sailor blouse but attach a double lace ruffle at the cuffs and create a double lace jabot. An additional pattern is included for the black bolero.

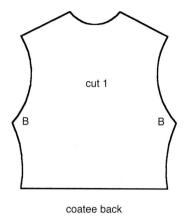

coatee back

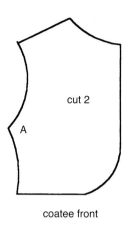

coatee front

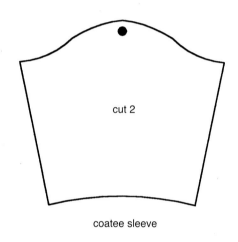

coatee sleeve

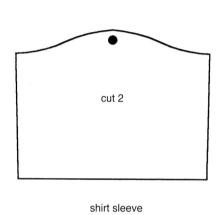

shirt sleeve

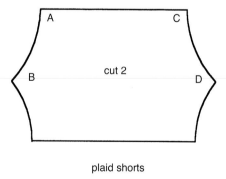

plaid shorts

sporran purse

Highland dress.

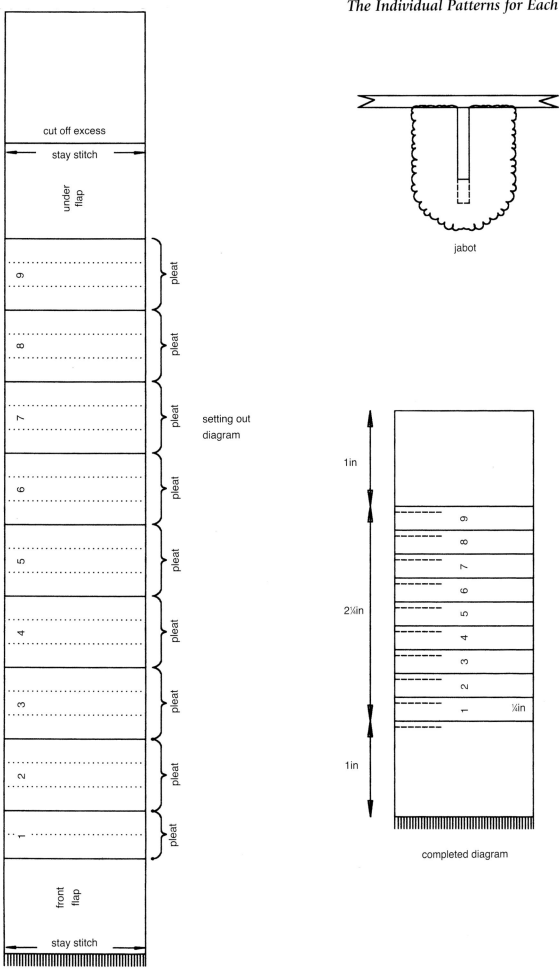

cut off excess

stay stitch

under flap

9 — pleat

8 — pleat

7 — pleat

setting out diagram

6 — pleat

5 — pleat

4 — pleat

3 — pleat

2 — pleat

1 — pleat

front flap

stay stitch

Highland dress.

jabot

1in

2¼in

9
8
7
6
5
4
3
2
1   ¼in

1in

completed diagram

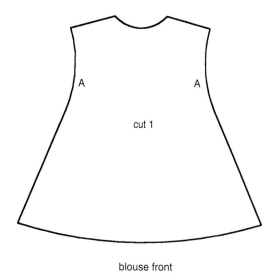

blouse front

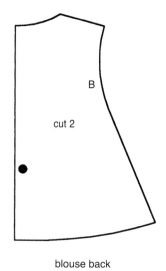

blouse back

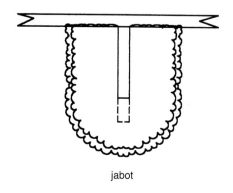

jabot

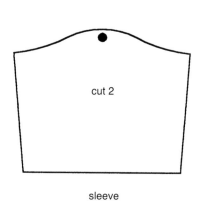

sleeve

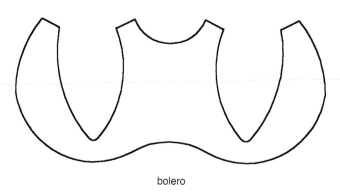

bolero

Girls' Highland dress.

The children in the nursery.

Bibliography

Anderson, J. and Garland, M. (revised by F. Kennet), *A History of Fashion* (Orbis, 1973)

Batterberry, M. and A., *Fashion: The Mirror of History* (Columbus, 1982)

Bray, N., *Dress Pattern Designing* (Granada, 1981)

Brook, I. and Laver, J., *English Costume of the Nineteenth Century* (A & C Black, 1929)

Brooke-Little, J.P., *Boutell's Heraldry* (Warne, 1973)

Burke, J., *An Illustrated History of England* (Book Club Associates, 1974)

Cassin-Scott, J., *The Illustrated Encyclopaedia of Costume and Fashion from 1066 to the Present* (Brockhampton Press, 1971)

Cunnington, P. and Buck, A., *Children's Costume in England* (A & C Black, 1965)

Ewing, E., *History of Children's Costume* (Batsford, 1977)

Granger, J., *Miniature Needlepoint Carpets* (Guild of Master Craftsmen, 1996)

Ingpen, R. and Wilkinson, P., *A Celebration of Customs and Rituals of the World* (Dragon's World, 1994)

Johnson, A., *How to Repair and Dress Old Dolls* (Bell, 1967)

Laver, J., *Children's Fashions in the Nineteenth Century* (Batsford, 1953)

Mass, J., *The Prince of Wales's Wedding: The Story of a Picture* (Cameron & Taylor/David & Charles, 1977)

Peacock, J., *Costume 1066–1990s* (Thames & Hudson, 1986)

Sichel, M., *History of Children's Costume* (Batsford, 1983)

Sichel, M., *History of Women's Fashion* (Batsford, 1984)

Index

Adidas 19
Alexandra 11, 33–9
aprons:
    cook 89, 93, 94
    household maids 96
    housekeeper 82–5

bodice 17–19, 30, 43, 47, 50, 58, 66, 79, 82, 85,
        89, 95, 100, 103, 112
    basque 33, 41, 50, 55
    construction of 31
body cover 12, 15
bolero 121
breeches 17, 79, 116
    patterns 81, 118
bride 11, 20, 32–3, 39, 43, 47
bridegroom 11
broderie anglaise 7, 18, 33, 96, 103
bustle 18, 33, 50, 53, 55
    pad 18, 55
butler 11, 12
    pattern 72–5

Camilla 11, 33
    pattern 106–8
caps 16, 17, 89, 94, 96, 97
children's patterns 100–24
Claire 11, 33
    pattern 112–13
coat 16–19, 30, 33, 58
    ceremonial 79
    frock 18, 33, 58, 59, 69
        pattern 64
    morning 33, 58, 59
        pattern 65
    tail 75, 79
        pattern 74, 81
coatee 119, 121
    pattern 122
collar 6, 16–18, 20, 39, 41, 55, 58, 66, 69
    sailor 113–16
    shawl 49, 50
    shirt 58, 72, 75, 116, 119
        pattern 63, 78, 118
Commodore 11, 33, 69
cook 11
    cuffs 94
    pattern 89–94

costume 20
    bride 33–9
    Duchess 47–50
    Duke 58–64
    Lady Osbourne 50–5
    Lady Victoria 55–7
    maid of honour 39–42
    Marchioness 43–6
    Marquis 58–65
cravat 58
crinoline 17, 20, 30, 33, 39, 40, 44, 47

Digby 11, 33
    pattern 116–19
dolls 6, 7, 11, 12, 20, 29, 30
    construction of 14
Duchess 11, 47–50
Duke 11, 58–64

epaulette 66

fashions 16–20, 29, 30, 116, 119
flounce 18, 20, 33, 34, 39, 40, 43, 44, 52, 53, 110

gardener 11
    pattern 75–9
governess 2, 11
    pattern 85–9
gown 16–18, 20, 31, 33
    bridal 33
    bustle 50, 55
    crinoline 39, 43, 47
groomsmen 11, 33, 58
    pattern 79–81

haberdashery 7
highland dress:
    boy's 119–23
    girl's 121–4
housekeeper 11, 12
    pattern 82–5

jabot 121
jacket 6, 17–19, 30, 33, 58, 116, 119
    butler 72
    casual 75, 79
    military 66
    naval 69

kilt 116, 119–21
    pattern 123
knickerbockers 18

leather 16–19, 66, 119, 121

maid:
    kitchen 11
        pattern 94–9
    nursery 11
        pattern 94–9
    parlour 11
        pattern 94–9
maid of honour 11, 39–42
Marchioness 11, 43–6
Marquis 11, 58–65
military uniform 33
    pattern 66–8

naval uniform 33, 58
    pattern 69–71
Nicholas 11, 33
    pattern 113–16
Nike 19
Norfolk suit 116

Osbourne
    Harriet 11, 33
        pattern 50–5
    twins 11, 116
        pattern 119–23
overskirt 17, 52–5

Pandora 11, 33
    pattern 103–5

pantaloons 30, 33, 39, 43, 44, 47, 48, 50, 55, 82,
    85, 89, 94, 100, 103, 107, 108, 112
petticoat 17, 18, 35, 39, 44, 47, 50, 55, 82, 85, 89,
    94–6, 100, 102, 103, 107, 108, 112
pinafore 33, 100, 103, 112

Reebok 19
ruffle 20, 50, 103, 107, 108, 112, 121

sailor suit 33, 113
shirt 16, 19, 30, 72, 75
    dress 58, 69
    sleeve 121
silk 7, 14, 16, 17, 31, 33, 50, 59, 75, 100, 107, 121
suit 18, 19, 33
    butler's 33, 72
    formal 33, 58

taffeta 31, 40, 59, 69, 72, 100, 121
toile 31, 58
trousers 16–19, 30, 33, 58, 59, 66, 69, 72,
    75, 113

Venetia 11, 33
    pattern 112–13
Verity 11, 33
    pattern 108–11
Victoria 11, 33
    pattern 55–7

wadding 14, 55
waistcoat 17, 59, 75, 79

yoke 6, 33, 100, 107, 108, 110